The GODHEAD

(REVISED)

By Kenneth V. Reeves

ISBN 0-912315-64-4

Cover Design by Tim Agnew

All Scripture quotations in this book are from the King James Version of the Bible unless otherwise identified.

Printed in the United States of America.

Seventh Edition

The Godhead (revised)

by Kenneth V. Reeves

Kenneth V. Reeves was born in 1922 on a farm in what is now known as the Shawnee National Forest former Indian Country, 7 miles south of Murphysboro, Illinois. The first 12 years of his life were spent in that country and in Granite City, Illinois. On January 20, 1938 he was converted, according to Acts 2:38, under the testimony of Robert D. Wolfe, his boyhood friend.

Reeves began to preach almost immediately and has continued for the past 46 years evangelizing, establishing new churches, and pastoring. He has pastored First United Pentecostal Church of Granite City, Illinois for the past 30 years.

TABLE OF CONTENTS

DEDICATION

This book is dedicated in fond and loving memory of my father, Joseph E. Reeves, who passed from this life to be with His Lord in the year of 1957. My father was a man of the Bible, and I trust that some of His knowledge of that book has come down to me. He was fond of saying "We have an unction from the holy ONE (Not Three) and know all things." May his soul forever rest in peace.

PREFACE

Sixth Edition

As far as I know, no writer has been able to write a book on the Godhead, to meet the approval of all readers. In fact most writers look back upon their writing with twenty-twenty vision wondering why they had not revised their material before the first printing. I am no different from the others as to this hindsight vision.

However, I did put in the preface of my book *The Godhead* published in 1962, that a revised edition might be used to improve or correct this book. And small additions have been added from time to time. This sixth edition is a revision of greater importance, in that the Word (John 1:1-3, 10, 14) is seen as in an Image as well as in Speech. The reader will notice the use of the words Word-Image and Verbal Word.

Now the Tri-God theorists say they believe in One God, but the books I have read from them in fact ends up in a Three God doctrine as much as Three Sheep are three sheep.

Yet One God theorists, in order to avoid the accusation to the effect that they are pluralistic in reference to God, bend all efforts to show that the One God is in Christ Jesus; which of course is true; but not all of the truth about God. And even though all One God people I know, realize that all of God's quantity is not deposited in the small body of the Savior; yet lack the language to identify and describe the same One God, Who is external to the body of Jesus.

Though this book expands its inquiry to include the rest of this One God, I maintain along with fellow One God believers, that there is only One Body in the Godhead: ''For in him dwelleth all the fulness of the Godhead bodily'' (Colossians 2:9). But I see that the form of God clothed Himself with the form of man, so that in Jesus dwells both the form of God and the form of man (Philippians 2:5-8).

Now the form of God has shape, but not organs, glands, or various systems as man who has bone, flesh, nerves, blood and respiratory systems as well as other factors such as color and weight. Angels are most nearly like God as to shape, except God's Shape or Image is Original and uncreated thus consists of another substance from that of angels. And inasmuch as Jesus is the image, shape or form of God inside His flesh and bone body (Luke 24:39, Colossians 1:15); and is also the Word, called God (John 1:1-3, 10, 14); then Jesus before the beginning, in the beginning, now and forever is the Word-Image; or now in the Incarnation, the Word-Image, in the image of man.

Thus in this revised edition of the Godhead, I feel it fair to expand, clarify, and revise the incomplete statement made in the previous edition: and distinguish God's Word-Image from God's speech or voice or spoken Word, which I call the Verbal-Word in this book.

But I end up with this statement: There is one God and one body in the godhead. (Colossians 2:9); and in this one body are two forms (morphes): The form of God within the form of man (Philippians 2:5-8).

PREFACE

(1962)

This is a book concerning the nature of the Godhead. Some words may be new to some readers, but a dictionary should be kept in easy reach for any such words. All possible questions have not been answered but many have been. Much light can be obtained by reading this book sincerely. The critic can find ways to construe what has been said in ways not intended by the writer. If a person does not really understand every point treated, he could show the courtesy of writing the author and asking him what is meant by some passages.

Words are vehicles of thought. Some failures may be discovered in the words chosen, but the fundamental ideas should be kept in mind; and the truth of the one true God should be believed as opposed to the pluralistic idea common today.

This is not the final word on this subject, as we know that there is much more to learn about God; but it is hoped by the author, in this edition, to contribute some light on the subject.

Therefore, in the sincere prayer that God, Who is all and in all, will lead us all to more of the truth about Himself, this book is submitted for your inspection.

This manuscript has been searched for possible errors of expression. It is possible some expressions are not as clear and accurate as the author would want. If afterwards the author discovers any such mistakes, perhaps a revised edition will clear it up. The basic positions will however, be maintained.

It is not the self-centered question "What do I think about God?" but the broader and to many the irritating question "What can be thought about God?"

INTRODUCTION

A book cannot fully express what should be said about the nature of the Godhead. For this reason, the reader may not find every question and answer that could have been given. There are also other facts and arguments that can easily be adduced in support of the main proposition of the book itself (Acts 17:24; John 1:3, 10).

But it is hoped that the nature of God, in general, might be more clearly seen, by viewing God specifically revealed in the flesh, and identified as Son of God. Jesus Christ is the God of that other world (or heaven) Who came into this world to give eternal life to as many as believed on Him (John 3:13).

There is no division between God in the world of flesh and the God outside of that world. . .but God in the world was in communion with His Omnipresence out of the world of flesh. Read John 17. Jesus Christ is the extension of the omnipresent and invisible God into the world of flesh. It is for this reason that the Spirit (Omnipresent Father) gave Him power (authority) over all flesh, giving eternal life to as many as the Father gave to Him.

God, in general, is a Spirit separate and apart from the flesh. God is also specifically in the flesh, yet He is not two beings, but one being. It is the same God in the world with God outside the world of flesh. God has an omnipresence and a particular presence.

The omnipresence of the Son is the Father. The particular residence of the Father in the flesh, is called the Son of God. Jesus said, "I and my Father are one" (John 10:30). The same God Who is exterior to Christ, is also internal in Christ (2 Corinthians 5:19).

The Godhead subject has been complicated by the adduction of such unbiblical phrases as God the Son, three separate and distinct persons in the Godhead and other such terms.

Take the following statements and see if they are in your Bible: God the Son; Trinity; three persons; God the Father, God the Son, and God the Holy Ghost; three separate and distinct persons.

If there are Three Separate and Distinct Persons, then all three are in Jesus; for He is the Son of God—He was full of the Holy Ghost, and He said, "My Father dwelleth in me." But because this idea of three separate and distinct persons breaks down, then a better identification and description of the Deity must be offered.

Therefore, this book attempts to show that the term "Person" or "Persons" is inadequate and misleading when used in reference to God. The term person is used in Hebrews 1:3 and is from the Greek word meaning substratum or "substance." The same Greek word is translated substance in Hebrews 11:1. "Now faith is the substance of things hoped for, the evidence of things not seen."

The word *person* is from a word that means *mask*. It was something worn by actors to portray a character. The only mask that God wore in the New Testament record, if one would call it a mask, is the flesh of Jesus Christ, by whom He lived as a man for the redemption of man (Hebrews 2). However, God was behind that mask or flesh of Jesus Christ. But I believe that the term *person* is not a term that should be used of God since it is a term derived from a mask on the face of an actor. The limited use that should be made of this could be when we speak of a human being.

If we divide God into persons, we are compelled to say that three persons also dwell in the New Testament Christians. Paul said that our bodies were temples of the Holy Ghost, that Jesus Christ was in us, and that the Father was in us also (1 Corinthians 6:19; 2 Corinthians 13:5; Ephesians 4:6).

Why would the Father and Son send the Holy Ghost if they were coming too? After all, Jesus said He was sending another Comforter called the Holy Ghost, and yet He and the Father are also in us. The simple truth is that God *outside* of Christ and God *inside* of Christ is the same. The Holy Ghost is that aspect of God that He promised to pour upon people or flesh, and is the Spirit of the Omnipresent Father. Jesus Christ, Who is man as well as God, is the channel through whom the Holy Ghost is given. John the Baptist said that Jesus would baptize you with the Holy Ghost and with fire.

This book attempts to break the barrier that was erected by those who apostated from the Apostolic Church, who added the term "Persons", in relation to the Bible terms of Father, Son and Holy Ghost. Men reason: The Son cannot be His own Father, therefore, they are two persons. However, God is not to be defined as a mask (person); but as an Omnipresent Spirit in His basic nature. He introduced Himself into this world from behind the veil or mask of human flesh—the seed of David. This manifestation of God was born of a woman. Being a male child, He was called Son. The distinction in Christ's Sonship from that of the human specie is that He is God fused with man.

As the reader will notice, God remained out of the world even if through the virgin birth He came into this world. The communion of God under such humiliating circumstances with God separate from that circumstance is deep calling unto deep. Jesus Christ is God with the assumed nature and likeness of men. He would therefore, pray as man even if His Divine Nature is the same as God in His "beyondness" from man.

The reader must always remember that God is One, not plural. So that the God in this world of sight, sound, and feeling speaks back to God in the world of Spirit. It is the same God existing under differing conditions and circumstances. What Scripture asserts that God is three? The Scripture affirms that these three are One, but not this One is three.

Christian Monotheism is not Trinitarianism. Trinitarianism is a merger of Tritheism (belief in Three Gods) with Monotheism (belief in One God), forming a hybrid doctrine, (a doctrine of mixed origin), which is neither Monotheism nor Tritheism in pure form. Many honest persons have been absorbed into the so-called Trinity without really knowing what the logical implications are. This is so, for it has been my pleasure to talk with so-called Trinity people, who confessed that what they believed about God was the same as what I believe.

They believe in the Father, Son and Holy Ghost and so do Christian Monotheists. They believe God is a Spirit, and that there is One God and so do Christian Monotheists. They believe that Jesus Christ is God manifest in the flesh, but that God is also Omnipresent Spirit as the Father and so do Christian Monotheists. They believe the Holy Ghost is God's Spirit that is promised by God to believers and so do Christian Monotheists. When they stop comparing God with persons, after the human analogy, these same dear people suddenly grasp the greater vision of the Godhead that is their right to enjoy. They suddenly discover that Christian Monotheists are expressing the truth that has only heretofore dwelt in them vaguely.

It is hoped that thousands of men and women will see that the mystery of the Trinity is the addition of the terms "Three Separate and Distinct Persons". It is hoped that the One God View will prevail among many, as they weigh the alternative herein offered.

Words are our best means to communicate, but words mean different things to different people. Words also serve to inform, argue and entertain. The Godhead is so profound that sermons and articles can only reveal certain aspects of the whole subject. For this reason, let the reader remember that Oneness ministers are seeking to establish Jesus Christ in His true Identity in contradistinction to Tritheism's attempt to make Him somebody else. We have perhaps erred in our zeal to establish His identity by our omission to describe and analyze the entire Deity in its quantitative as well as its qualitative aspects. Please pardon our zeal if we have previously omitted the other aspects of the unlimited God.

Read with patience, understanding and pray that God will assist you in your study of this book.

You will be interested in how God made Himself visible in Christ. The way God made the visible and invisible worlds was through His Word-Image in the beginning. All of God's acts were wrought through His Word-Image by whom the worlds were made. Through the virgin birth the Word-Image was made flesh and tented or tabernacled among us in Jesus Christ. The worlds were made and upheld by the spoken word that issued out through the Word-Image. As the Word is God expressed, so is the Word made flesh,

God made visible. It was God who looked out on a world of flesh through the eyes of Jesus Christ. The Word is both in image form and in verbal form as revealed in the man Christ Jesus.

As the Word is God expressed, so the Word made flesh is God revealed or made visible. I repeat, it was God Who looked out upon the world of flesh through the eyes of Jesus Christ.

The Word in Image Form with the Verbal Word were revealed in the man Christ Jesus.

The Holy Ghost descended upon the man Christ Jesus, by which He was anointed Prophet, King, Priest and Mediator. God was fused with man in the virgin birth, and the child shall be called the Son of God. Just as God made Himself visible by the fusion of the Word and flesh, the same God anointed Jesus of Nazareth with the Holy Ghost at His baptism by John (Matthew 3:17; Acts 10:38). This Holy Ghost with which He was full (Luke 4:1) is the Father aspect that Jesus said dwelt in Him (John 14:10); yet, the Father, larger than a single body was still in heaven and is above all, through all and in you all at the same time (Ephesians 4:6).

The Father is God in His most universal sense. The Son of God is God in manifestation or particularly revealed in the flesh. The Holy Ghost is God imparting Himself to mankind in one way or another (or God in the church in this dispensation), i.e. God in the universe, God in Christ, and God in the church. The one God in all three spheres, but not three Gods or three persons. If the reader will see that the man-made mystery of the Trinity should be changed to the mystery of God, even Christ, a great step forward will have been made.

The term fusion as used in this book is not to be interpreted to mean that the divine nature and human nature of Jesus have been lost or confused or made identical, but rather alloyed. God did not irretrievably lose His identity in the process of incarnation. Read last chapter.

ONE GOD

IS THERE ONE GOD?

"Hear, O Israel: The LORD our God is one LORD" (Deuteronomy 6:4 and Mark 12:29).

"Thou shalt have no other gods before me" (Exodus 20:3).

"Is there a God beside me? yea, there is no God; I know not any" (Isaiah 44:8).

"Hath not one God created us?" (Malachi 2:10).

"Now a mediator is not a mediator of one, but God is one" (Galatians 3:20).

"Thou believest that there is one God; thou doest well: the devils also believe, and tremble" (James 2:19).

To the question as to whether there is One God, the Bible affirmatively answers YES! Paul affirmed that a mediator was not a mediator of one, but God is one. That is while a mediator stands in the middle between two or more contending parties, yet God was one, not two or more.

Paul again said, "For there is one God, and one mediator between God and men, the man Christ Jesus" (1 Timothy 2:5).

All who believe the Bible must believe in One God—for God is One (Galatians 3:20).

GOD and gods

IS GOD ONE OR THREE?

This is perhaps the most basic question in or out of the universe. Ditheists say there are two Gods and Tritheists say there are three Gods. Trinitarians say there is one God in three separate and distinct persons. Monotheists, other than Christian Monotheists say there is one God. Christian Monotheists say there is one God Who has revealed Himself in three basic ways, but is not divided into persons after the analogy of the human specie.

WHAT IS THE TRITHEISTIC VIEW?

Tritheism is a belief in three gods with separate and distinct existences.

WHAT IS THE TRINITARIAN CONCEPT?

The doctrine of the Trinity is that God is one God subsisting in three separate and distinct persons. They confess that this is a mystery above reason but not contrary to reason. They do not all say that these three persons have a body, but they have all the attributes that define a person to be a person, which they say does not always mean that a body is involved.

WHAT IS DITHEISM?

Ditheism is a belief in two Gods. Some of this belief partakes of the nature of God in an uncreated sense, creating the Son of God in the beginning, who in turn by delegated authority created all things that are made. This is believed to be the origin of the Son of God in the Sonship relationship. This means to the so-called Ditheist that this is the origin of the created Son, but not His origin as God, in the uncreated sense. The impression one gets is of a Senior and Junior God.

WHAT IS MONOTHEISM?

Monotheism is the ancient doctrine that God is One, not many. It is succinctly summarized by the verse: "Hear, O Israel: The LORD our God is one LORD" (Deuteronomy 6:4). This is the extreme opposite of a plurality of beings whether called Tritheism or even Tritheism in its modified form termed Trinity. It is this fundamental belief that is the root and branch of Jewish rejection of the Trinitarianism and Tritheism of the so-called Christian world, for they feel that their Messiah will be the one God of the Old Testament coming in the form of man.

WHAT IS CHRISTIAN MONOTHEISM?

It is the same as Jewish Monotheism with the exception that the Son of God is the Messiah, and that this One God has sent His Spirit in and upon the people as the Holy Ghost. There is One God Who lives in and out of the universe as the source of all things, yet Who also assumed the human nature of man through Mary, within which His divine form and nature were fused and called the Son of God in relation to divine origin and present dwelling in the flesh; and also called the Son of Man in relation to His human origin and dwelling in the flesh; with the added manifestation of Himself under the appellation of the Holy Ghost or Spirit dwelling and being imparted in and to the lives of believers in Jesus Christ.

IS IT ACCURATE TO SAY THAT CHRISTIAN MONOTHEISTS ARE JESUS ONLY?

NO! Christian Monotheists believe that Jesus Christ is God made visible through incarnation, but that God is basically an Omnipresent Spirit Substance, whose Absolute Being transcends even the universe as an unlimited existence. Although Jesus Christ is the One God of the Old Testament, He is not all there is to God as to quantity, speaking from the standpoint of the size of the body.

The idea may be conveyed in a rough analogy by the use of water and ice:

Ice is of water, and may be in water, but is water in a solid form. Jesus is God in human form, but God is an omnipresent Spirit, too. As Jesus said concerning His connection with God in this Spirit sense, "I am in the Father and the Father is in me." Ice is in the water and the water is in the ice. "I and my Father are one." The Holy Ghost is sometimes called the Spirit of my Father and the Spirit of God's Son. This analogy is imperfect, since God assumed the flesh and life of man in order to live and move among men; and is not Spirit converted to flesh.

IS IT ACCURATE TO SAY THAT CHRISTIAN MONOTHEISTS DENY THE FATHER?

This has been told and retold but is highly inaccurate and misleading. The Christian Monotheist simply denies that God should be characterized under the appellation of three separate and distinct persons, whether under the extreme Tritheistic concept or the modified Tritheistic concept commonly called Trinity. Christian Monotheists believe that when God is referred to as Father, He is being addressed as the source from whence all things originated. When the One God of the Bible assumed a mode of Being in the flesh, this distinct manifestation of Himself originated from God in the sense of Spirit. The Spirit Substance, which is eternal and omnipresent, is the source or Father of the fusion of God and man in one body and called the Son of God. This Fatherhood of the Spirit has carried over and been applied to Jesus when His Deity or divine nature or substance is being identified, and/or emphasized more in particular, in contradistinction to His humanity. Thus, when His substance, which is the same as the Spirit, is preeminently in mind, Jesus Christ is also identified as God or WORD. In His Deity Jesus, in the body, is One or the same as the Deity outside of the body. When viewed as being the product of a fusion of the divine and the human, the appellation of Son of God and Son of Man are used. Unlike Tritheism or Trinitarianism, Christian Monotheism includes the whole Deity in an Undivided Substance, rather than to project a troika (three) of separated individuals or council of persons like to the unity that perhaps three people may form—a unity though plural. Christian Monotheism includes both the God of infinity in His Unlimited Omnipresence as a Spirit Substance, and also this Substance expressed in human form; thus fusing, as it were, the Divine Nature and the human nature. God is, therefore, to be understood from two senses: God apart from the flesh and God manifested in the flesh. Again the analogy of water and ice: The water is in the ice and the ice is in the water (ice in the lake and the lake in the ice).

Monotheism (belief in One God) is a Oneity not a Trinitarian Unity. The Trinitarian Unity is a United Council of Three Persons in sociological agreement. The

Monotheistic Oneity is One Being made known in various ways, degrees and quantities, etc.

JESUS ONLY?

WHAT TRUTH IS THERE IN THE CHARGE THAT THE PEOPLE WHO HAVE BEEN CALLED ONENESS PENTECOSTAL ARE JESUS ONLY?

This charge is partly based on the notion that the so-called One God Church excludes the rest of God from the Godhead when the statement is made that Jesus is the one true God of the Bible. However, the fact that Jesus is God does not mean that the total quantity of Deity is enclosed or encased within the small body of the Savior. It simply means that the total quality of the Godhead resides in Jesus from a bodily standpoint—that His is the only body in the Godhead—that there is not another separated body. "For in him dwelleth all the fulness of the Godhead bodily" (Colossians 2:9). The statement of Jesus Only, in the sense of limiting the total quantity of God to the body of Jesus is, therefore, an inaccurate description; and does not fit the One God doctrine of the Christian Monotheist.

SHOULD THE TERM "PERSON" BE USED TO DESCRIBE THE GODHEAD?

For sometime this writer has felt that the use of the human term *person* or *persons* should be excluded from the definition of God. The term is used to identify human beings, and is not used of lower creatures such as monkeys or higher creatures such as angels. A disservice has been done by calling God or any part of God "Person". The very word is derived from the word *mask* and perhaps got its origin from the actors who wore masks to portray different characters. If the term *person* is to be retained, let it be limited to Jesus Christ in His humanity as the Son of Man. This may be permitted on the grounds that He was truly a man in His humanity, and it might not be too imprecise to term Jesus by the word *person*. Even at that, it seems that this should be carefully defined and carefully construed.

BUT DOES NOT THE SCRIPTURE RECORD THAT JESUS IS THE EXPRESS IMAGE OF HIS (God's) PERSON?

The King James Version of the Bible translates as follows: "Who [Jesus] being the brightness of his [God's] glory, and the express image of his [God's] person, . . ." (Hebrews 1:3). The revised version is: the very image of his substance. The term *image* is from the Greek word *character,* and the word *express* is *impressed.* Jesus is the *impressed character of God's substance. God's substance was expressed in the flesh—Paul said, "God was manifest in the flesh" (1 Timothy 3:16).*

DOES NOT PAUL SAY THAT IF HE FORGAVE "FORGAVE I IT IN THE PERSON OF CHRIST?"

In 2 Corinthians 2:10 Paul used the words "The person of Christ." As said in a previous answer, the term person may be qualifiedly used of Jesus if His identity as a man is intended. Of course, as is known, the King James Version of the Bible contains many terms that are not used today in the same sense. One may translate and say "with the approval of Christ I forgive" or "in His presence" or "on His behalf." At any rate, the term *person* has now taken to itself such a specific content in ordinary speech that it should more fittingly be limited to the human family or specie.

WOULD THE TERMS THERE IS ONE GOD AND ONE BODY IN THE GODHEAD BE MORE READILY UNDERSTOOD?

Yes, because the confusion that exists now, as to just what qualities are required to constitute a person, is perhaps too great to convey a proper concept of Jesus being God in a Body. The scriptures in other places, where God in a Body is not the subject, describe God as One—as being Spirit as to substance—of existing everywhere or omnipresent. This fully describes that the One God of the Bible is bigger than the frame, form or image of Jesus Christ. Hence, the total Deity can be described whether in respect to a particular Body or in general as an Omnipresent Spirit. So by saying that there is One God and One Body, (containing two forms i.e. the form of God and the form of man) in the Godhead the concrete position of the Christian Monotheist is more clearly stated.

HAS THE ADDITION OF THE TERMS THREE PERSONS BEEN AN ASSET IN UNDERSTANDING THE GODHEAD?

Not really, although, that is the proposed reason for the adoption of the terms. The Bible does not say that God is Three Persons, but that God is One. Even though such terms as Father, Son, and Holy Ghost are freely used, the term "Three Persons" (or three masks) was not used by Bible writers. The reason is obvious once we fully understand that God is not related within Himself as human beings are; in a sociological sense. For instance, the Father is in the Lord Jesus (John 14:10). The Lord Jesus is in the Father (John 14:11, 12). The Father is in Christians, the Son is in Christians, and the Holy Ghost is in Christians. Actually, the Holy Ghost is the one who is in us as can be shown later. So, for the present, eliminate the Gentile definition of God into person or persons as too misleading. We will be able to describe more of the details of the Godhead by using other terms.

SPIRIT AND WORD

INTO WHAT ASPECTS CAN GOD'S NATURE OR SUBSTANCE BE ANALYZED OR INTO WHAT TWO ELEMENTS IS IT POSSIBLE TO ANALYZE THE BASIC NATURE OF GOD?

The answer is: Spirit and Word.

Jesus gave us the essence of God in its most ultimate sense when He said, "God is a Spirit" (John 4:24). However, John the beloved in this same Gospel said, "In the beginning was the Word, and the Word was with God, and the Word was God. The same was in the beginning with God" (John 1:1-2). There is One God, and God is One; but here the Word is identified as God, and is with God. How can these things be?

The key to this question is the term *beginning*. This is the origin of time and of God's identification in relation to time. This is the connection of God to the creation of heaven and earth as is found in Genesis 1:1, "In the beginning God created the heaven and the earth," and "All things were made by him [the Word]; and without him [the Word] was not any thing made that was made" (John 1:3).

Hence, the God Who had no beginning connected Himself to time and creation by means of the Word. David said, "Before the mountains were brought forth, or ever thou hadst formed the earth and the world, even from everlasting to everlasting, thou art God" (Psalm 90:2).

So, this second element enters into the question— ". . .and the Word was with GOD, and the Word was GOD." The Spirit is the ultimate essence that makes up God, yet the Word, which is God's essence expressed, reveals God. It is the way that a timeless God related Himself to time.

The term *Word* means logic, wisdom, plan, purpose, speech, etc. It is from the Greek word "Logos." Hence, God made all things by His Word, or wisdom, or plan; and by speaking these things into existence through His Word-Image.

To sum up, the Word is God related to the beginning of the heaven and the earth and the creation thereof. The Word is God in time. But to forestall the belief that the God Who has stepped out of eternity into time is two Beings, John said that the Word that was with God, was God; and is the same God as the God related to eternity—One God, related to time as the Word, but as ever a God related to that vast eternity before time and creation.

The relation of the Word to the Spirit is that of channel, cause, and means. The Spirit is the force that is behind the word. The word is the means, but the Spirit is the force using the means.

WHAT DID ADAM CLARK HAVE TO SAY?

"Logos, which signifies a word spoken, speech eloquence, doctrine, reason or the faculty of reasoning is very properly applied to Him, Who is the true light which lighteth every man who cometh into the world."

"AND THE WORD WAS GOD"—or God was the Logos, and therefore no subordinate being—no second to the most high, but the supreme eternal Jehovah.

"ALL THINGS WERE MADE BY HIM"—that is by this Logos. In Genesis 1:1 God is said to have created all things. In this verse, Christ is said to have created all things. The same unerring Spirit spoke in Moses and in the evangelists. Therefore, Christ and the Father are One. To say that Christ made all things by a delegated power from God is absurd because the thing is impossible. Creation means causing that to exist that had no previous being. This is evidently a work that can be effected only by omnipotence. Now, God cannot delegate His omnipotence to another. If this were possible, he to whom this omnipotence was delegated would, in consequence, become God; and he from whom it was delegated would cease to be such. It is impossible that there should be two omnipotent beings. On these two important passages I find that many imminently learned men differ from me. It seems that they cannot be of my opinion, and I feel I cannot be of theirs. May He Who is the Light and Truth guide them and myself into all truth!

"And dwelt among us"—(John 1:14) or, and tabernacled among us in the human nature which He took of the virgin."

SINCE THE WORD IS VERBAL WHEN SPOKEN, IS THE SAME WORD IN BODY OR SHAPE FORM, WHEN EXPRESSED IN JESUS CHRIST?

"By the word of the LORD were the heavens made; and all the host of them by the breath of his mouth. . .For he spake, and it was done" (Psalm 33:6, 9).

"Through faith we understand that the worlds were framed by the word of God" (Hebrews 11:3).

But when the Word was made flesh, the Word was heard, seen, looked upon and handled. This Word existed in an Image as well as being verbal.

"That which was from the beginning, which we have heard, which we have seen with our eyes, which we have looked upon, and our hands have handled, of the Word of life" (1 John 1:1).

One writer speaks of the full-orbed Deity of Jesus Christ. He is the Light of the World, and His Word is the outbeaming of Himself in act and speech.

GOD MANIFEST IN THE FLESH

WHAT IS IT THAT MUST BE KEPT IN MIND WHEN VIEWING JESUS CHRIST AS GOD MANIFEST IN THE FLESH?

It must always be remembered that when God assumed

the form and nature of man and became a servant (Philippians 2:6-8), the Self-Imposed limits were so real that Jesus was the weakness of God, and the Gospel He preached was the foolishness of God (1 Corinthians 1:25). Do not forget that God was putting on no act when He assumed, in particular, those limits that belong to man. God lived under the conditions and circumstances of men, in the Incarnation. The veil of flesh served as more than a shield between Himself and man. That veil limited God, to a great degree, within the body. He knew much more in His Omnipresence, Omniscience and Omnipotence outside of the body. God in the assumed likeness and limits of man prayed for us and also spoke of the Glory that was stripped from Him in the Incarnation (John 17).

Even the miracles He did are, in effect, duplicated by His disciples—Peter also walked on the water. Jesus Christ is God reduced to such proportions that God has stooped as low as He can and yet remain God in the earth. However, God did not shortchange Jesus Christ as to His relationship to us in respect to wisdom, righteousness, sanctification and redemption (1 Corinthians 1:30).

God in a particular place is only Omniscient in relation to God in all other places. God in a particular place is also only Omnipresent in relation to God in all other places. Again, God is only Omnipotent in relation to God in His entirety. Jesus is God's only body, and in the resurrection, the weakness of God as caused by the flesh is largely, if not altogether, removed by the immortality given the flesh thereby. He was crucified in weakness but raised in power. God in particular has by the resurrection of the physical body, been restored to the glory He had before the world began. His contact with God in His Omnipresence, Omniscience and Omnipotence is not encumbered with the weakness and limitations to which the virgin birth had surrounded Him. The super-injection of the God-life did not destroy His humanity in the resurrection, but it caused the humanity He assumed to take on immortality.

The incarnation limited Him as God when viewed within that particular body. The resurrection from the dead unlimited Him to God, Omnipresent and exterior to that particular body. Also, it must not be forgotten that God within the body is the same, being as God exterior to the body. The distinction is the particularity of the bodily manifestation from the generality or non-bodily manifestation. Jesus said, "I and my Father are one" (John 10:30).

To further illustrate the point: The Holy Ghost in Peter was God, but surely not all of God, since the other eleven also had the Holy Ghost. Not only the twelve had the Holy Ghost, but many others received the Holy Ghost then and later. While the Holy Ghost in each of us is One with the rest of God elsewhere, yet the particular God in us only knows that aspect of knowledge within its orbit when viewed within the context of the human life. Being part of the total God, the Holy Ghost in each one has an unlimited aspect exterior to that particular human life.

The difference, however, in Jesus Christ is that He is God fused in and with man through the virgin birth, and we are men anointed with the Holy Ghost after having been born of a natural father and mother. His very Being is a fusion of God and man, while ours is the engrafting of the Word in our lives and the coming of God by impartation in the Holy Ghost. It is true that the Holy Ghost descended upon Jesus, and He was said to have been full of the Holy Ghost. However, as truly man as well as God, He had various offices to fill and had to be anointed as Prophet, Priest and King.

INTERNAL RELATIONSHIP OF GOD

DOES A PLURALITY CONFUSE THE DOCTRINE OF ONE GOD? WHAT IS A MEDIATOR?

No, not just a plurality, but a plurality of Gods or Persons creates a problem. The variety in God is manifold. In short, the teaching of One God becomes confused only when people admit into the argument such unbiblical additions as Three Persons or Trinity of Persons. The very language is a repudiation of the Bible. As long as those terms and their implications are admissable in the discussion, as even having a decent origin, there will be a thick cloud of unnecessary mystery covering the human race from now on.

WHAT IS A MEDIATOR?

The word *mediator* means a middle man or go-between. It is the man Christ Jesus Who is called the mediator between God and men. Paul said, "For there is one God, and one mediator between God and men, the man Christ Jesus" (1 Timothy 2:5).

In Galatians 3:20 Paul again said, "Now a mediator is not a mediator of one, but God is one."

Men are many. A mediator must have at least two parties to serve as a go-between. But while a mediator must have two or more parties to be a middle man, God is not two or three or more—God is one. It is the *man* Christ Jesus, not the God Christ Jesus who is the mediator.

WHEN WE SPEAK OF THE OMNIPRESENCE OF GOD, WHO OR WHAT DO WE IDENTIFY OR DESCRIBE?

The Omnipresence of God is primarily known as the Father. Paul said, "One God and Father of all, who is above all, and through all, and in you all" (Ephesians 4:6).

DOES THE SON OF GOD HAVE OMNIPRESENCE?

Yes. The Omnipresence of the Son of God is His Father. There can only be One Omnipresence, and this One Spirit, called the Father, is the Omnipresence of the Son of God. This is why the Father was in the Son, and the Son was in the Father. This is why Jesus could be in heaven and still be on earth (John 3:13).

DOES THE HOLY GHOST HAVE OMNIPRESENCE?

The answer is yes, in the same way that the Son has Omnipresence. The Holy Ghost is the Spirit of God designated to inspire and fill mankind. As Jesus said, "But when they deliver you up, take no thought how or what ye shall speak: for it shall be given you in that same hour what ye shall speak. For it is not ye that speak, but the Spirit of your Father which speaketh in you'' (Matthew 10:19, 20).

The Holy Ghost is addressed as He and Him, just as any particular aspect of God is God and should be addressed as an intelligent Being. When God incarnate speaks of that portion of God that is to come into believers, He calls the Spirit or Holy Ghost He and Him. The actual fact is: The Holy Ghost is a portion of the Father proceeding from Him into our lives. The Godhead must not be divided. On the day of Pentecost Peter told them and us plainly that the Holy Ghost is the Spirit of God: ''And it shall come to pass in the last days, saith God, I will pour out of my Spirit upon all flesh'' (Acts 2:17). The Holy Ghost in the believer is called by various terms: ''the Spirit of God dwelleth in you'' (1 Corinthians 3:16); ''your body is the temple of the Holy Ghost'' (1 Corinthians 6:19); ''as God hath said I will dwell in them'' (2 Corinthians 6:16). In 2 Corinthians 13:5 Paul told the Corinthians to examine themselves to see whether or not they were in the faith—to determine if Jesus Christ was in them. The Holy Ghost is God's particular presence in and for believers, and otherwise to deal with mankind. This particular presence is of the Omnipresence.

IS THERE ANY INTERNAL COMMUNICATION WITHIN THE GODHEAD IN THE SENSE THAT GOD IN ONE PLACE MAY SPEAK OF OR EVEN TO GOD IN ANOTHER PLACE?

It would not be surprising that this should be found true. The size of God being what it is, and the multi-intelligence that He possesses, and the manifold interests that He has, all congregate to indicate that there is a vast internal communication within God. The intercession of the Spirit within believers (Romans 8:26, 27) indicates some form of communication. How this is carried on is left almost entirely God's own secret. But plurality of persons is certainly not the answer. God in a particular place can speak, and God in all places may speak. Remember on the day of Pentecost how the Spirit of the Omnipresent God came into about one hundred and twenty persons at once, and they all spoke as the Spirit gave them utterance. God can speak through many persons—out of a cloud—out of heaven, or any place; but it will all relate to Jesus Christ, The Word made flesh.

IS "THE WORD" FORM AND SPEECH OF THE GODHEAD AND "THE SPIRIT" THE QUANTITY OF THE GODHEAD?

This may be the best way to express the mystery. God in His basic nature is an Omnipresent Spirit. He expressed Himself by His Word-Image to create heaven and earth. The Word expressed the qualities of Divine Power, wisdom and authority. Throughout the Old Testament God made Himself known by His Word through and to various individuals. He even appeared in various forms or images so that the Word could be conveyed to the eye and ear. Certain persons such as Moses, David, Melchizedek and the prophets also typified and illustrated the Word. Even the tabernacle built by Moses was a type or object lesson of the Word by implication. God's Word, whether in creation, promise, prophecy, or precept or as typified by the holy men, the tabernacle and sacrifices, was made flesh and dwelt among us in the body of the Lord Jesus Christ. This quality of God called the Word holds the universe together, and is embodied in Christ and is written in the Bible. The Word is the expression of God's power, wisdom and authority.

It is God revealed in power and authority. This Word, when spoken of respecting the beginning and the incarnation, is the Word; and the God made known in the beginning by creation became the God of redemption in the incarnation.

THE WORD

IF THE WORD IS GOD QUALITATIVELY SPEAKING DOES THE WORD HAVE A REAL EXISTENCE?

The answer is: The Word is God in time and creation. It appears that God in time and creation is as real as God outside of time and creation. The Word is God revealed. It is God in His Self Revealings, whether in Creation, in prophecy, in promise or in any way that He has made Himself known in truth. In a sense we may say it is God externalizing Himself in and/or through matter.

Even the body of Jesus Christ is matter and was created or was of created matter from the virgin Mary. This is the Word or God in His closest Self Revelation through something created.

The Word is not created matter. It is the form and verbal expression of God in creation and in redemption through His Image-Word. Angels are substances but not of matter as we think of things terrestrial—but rather of things celestial. There are celestial bodies and bodies terrestrial. The Word-Image is God's uncreated invisible shape.

Verily, it was not the nature or substance of angels that God as Word, or God in Self Revelation, took in Jesus

Christ, but the seed or substance of Abraham (Hebrews 2). This merger of Word and matter is called the Son of God—Son of Man.

From His human nature it would necessarily be that He is God's Created Son (He partook of a fleshly nature from Mary's side). From the Divine Nature He is Creator since all things were made by Him. Hence, the Sonship arises through the birth; and it is the Son in His Humanity Who was capable of dying in the flesh. But Jesus was more than man. He was Creator-Word, and in Him is and was eternal life.

The great mystery remains even after knowledge is obtained. God in His Fatherhood and Omnipresence lingers in the background as the force behind this Self-Revelation. He is described as being above, in, and through all these Self-Revelations. So that no matter how much He has made Himself known in creation and as Creator turned Redeemer in Christ, there is that Omnipresent Remoteness of the Everlasting God that the Self-Revelations identify and declare. Although it is God Who has made Himself known in the Creation of all things and has called this Revelation of Himself "the Word", yet the Word and the effects of the Word all go to identify, analyze and describe the God Who remained the same invisible, unlimited and unsearchable Being of infinity as if He had never made Himself known. These are the two sides of Deity.

The Word is, may we say, God outwardly expressed. The Father is the same God as the Source of that Expression. The Father is the Spirit that expressed the Word. It was the LORD God that made the earth and the heavens (Genesis 2:4), and it is the LORD (JEHOVAH) GOD Who tented among us in Jesus Christ.

THE FATHER IS IN THE SON

BUT WHERE DOES THE FATHER DWELL?

"But the Father that dwelleth in me, he doeth the works" (John 14:10).

"As thou, Father, art in me" (John 17:21).

"That ye may know, and believe, that the Father is in me" (John 10:38).

This is at least three times that Jesus said that the Father dwelt in Him.

Paul said to the Corinthians Church, "To wit, that God was in Christ" (2 Corinthians 5:19).

If the Holy Ghost is a separate person from the Father, how do we reconcile the following scripture: "And Jesus being full of the Holy Ghost" (Luke 4:1).

The only rational way to reconcile it is when God comes into a body or moves upon human beings, He describes Himself as the Holy Ghost. In this way He distinguishes the particular type of manifestation from other kinds. However, Jesus labels the Holy Ghost as the same Spirit as the Father since God is one and is the One Spirit.

If my reader will abandon for the time being the separation of God into what amounts to three divine people, or persons, and will read carefully from Matthew 1:18, 20, one cannot help knowing that the Holy Ghost is that part of the Father that overshadowed Mary and actuated the conception of Jesus. "Now the birth of Jesus Christ was on this wise: When as his mother Mary was espoused to Joseph, before they came together, she was found with child of the

Holy Ghost. . . .But while he [Joseph] thought on these things, behold, the angel of the Lord appeared unto him in a dream, saying, Joseph thou son of David, fear not to take unto thee Mary thy wife: for that which is conceived in her is of the Holy Ghost'' (Matthew 1:18, 20).

The Father dwelt in the Son—dwelt in heaven, and through all, and Paul said "in you all." The Father being Omnipresent is particularly present in Jesus Christ.

THE SON IS IN THE FATHER

HOW CAN THE FATHER DWELL IN THE SON IF THE SON IS IN THE FATHER?

"Believest thou not that I am in the Father" (John 14:10).

"And I in thee" (John 17:21).

The last chapter tells us that the Father was in the Son. This chapter tells us that the Son is in the Father. How can the Father and the Son be in each other?

An analogy may be drawn from ice and water. In the ocean there may be an iceberg. The iceberg is made out of water and floats in the water. The ice is another form of water. In the similarity thus indicated, it is suggested that Jesus is God in the form of man, and that He is in the Father or Spirit as the iceberg is in the water. Just as the ice is in the water, yet it is from water that the iceberg is formed.

It is water in two forms, liquid and solid. We are not eliminating the Father from the Godhead equation but describing by words the nature of the relationship.

To unite Jesus Christ to God rather than divide Him from God, note the following scriptures:

"God was manifest in the flesh" (1 Timothy 3:16).

"For unto us a child is born, unto us a son is given: and the government shall be upon his shoulder: and his name shall be called Wonderful, Counsellor, The mighty God, The everlasting Father, The Prince of Peace" (Isaiah 9:6).

Since there is one God and the Lord Jesus is identified as God, it is necessary to say that Jesus Christ is this God in the form of a visible man. You will carefully see how that the writer designates Jesus to be God in a bodily sense, but with the provision that God still retains His basic Spirit nature universally dwelling or Omnipresent.

"For in him [Jesus] dwelleth all the fulness of the Godhead bodily" (Colossians 2:9). That is, all the qualities of the Godhead dwelleth in Jesus Christ. This is not to say that all the quantity of the Godhead dwelleth in the body of Jesus Christ. All that God is "qualitatively" is embodied and expressed in Jesus Christ. Jesus is the "Brightness of God's glory, and the express image of His [God's] person [or Substance]" (Hebrews 1:3). From a bodily standpoint, Jesus is God in a body. The word "substance" is more accurate than person since the same Greek Word is translated substance in Hebrews 11:1. Hence, the divine substance is imaged forth in Jesus Christ.

INFERIORITY

WAS JESUS ON EARTH IN ANY WAY INFERIOR TO THE FATHER?

By defining the Father as Omnipresent Spirit and the Son of God as that merger of God and man, there would be some loss by the Incarnation, viewing Jesus in His entirety as having human parts as well as Divine. Perhaps brass is somewhat less than pure copper due to zinc added. However, just as the copper in the brass may have its identity less identifiable because of the other ingredients, yet the copper in the brass is copper just as much as copper in its pure and separated state. So the Divinity in Jesus Christ is as much God as God apart from this body, yet the Divinity was more difficult to ascertain, joined as it was with His humanity.

His inferiority in the flesh and under the conditions and circumstances of the Incarnation is due to the purpose of His coming, the limits of the body and the subjection to the Father (Omnipresent Spirit), Who also dwelt within Him. Anyone viewing the limited confines to which Jesus was subjected in the earth will, on the face of it, see that He is God particularly adapting Himself to the confines of human life.

There is no inferiority in Jesus Christ in His Undivided Deity as God. He is the same as the Father. The Father came to head in Jesus Christ. The Father emerges out of invisibility in Jesus Christ (John 14:7-10). Therefore, just because Jesus is God concretely and particularly revealed in a body, in no way separates the Father from the Son, as it would among humans. Rather, God particularized

Himself in the flesh, and Father and Son are fitting terms to describe God in His Omnipresent and eternal aspect from the particular aspect into which He projected Himself.

EQUALITY

WHAT IS THE EQUALITY OF JESUS CHRIST WITH GOD?

Tritheism seeks to establish a co-equal status of Three Divine Persons in the Godhead, and any scripture that seems to bear out a plurality is seized with utmost relish and squeezed for every bit of support for the Tritheistic position.

The equality that Jesus had with God was that everything that has been said about God has also been attributed to Jesus Christ. Since there cannot be two or more Supreme Beings, God, in the Form or Image, must possess the attributes of omnipresence, omnipotence, omniscience, immutability and eternality exterior to that form. The Father, Who is this omnipresence, omnipotence, immutability, omniscience and eternality, must also have the attribute of that form or image. In short, the form of God possesses all the attributes of the Father, and the Father possesses that form or image as His attribute.

This way all that the Father is belongeth to Jesus Christ and Jesus Christ is the Father's Image (John 5:37) inside the image of man. Hence, Jesus said, "I and my Father are One" (John 10:30).

"Now the Father is greater than I", Jesus said (John

14:28). This is not the equality of the Tritheist. There is One Deity, and He is the Father in His Unlimited Presence, but this same Deity is imaged forth in the image of man and named Jesus (or Jehovah). God in Christ is the same as God exterior to Christ. He is the same One under different conditions and circumstances. Hence, being in the Form of God makes Him equal to Himself beyond and outside of Form. It is the same Supreme Being. Jesus is God's Bright Glory—He is God's character impressed in the Lord Jesus Christ, so that "He that seeth me seeth the Father," Jesus said (John 14).

Jesus is the visible expression of the invisible God. In taking the form of a servant His status under that condition is less than the Father.

GOD IS UNLIMITED

HOW BIG, STRONG AND WISE IS GOD? DOES HE HAVE ANY LIMITS?

God is *unlimited* as to size, knowledge and power. A circle cannot be drawn large enough to encompass God. There is not anything but that God already knows it. He is so powerful that the words "Almighty" and "Omnipotent" are ascribed as belonging to Him.

This implies that God is omnipresent, omniscient and omnipotent—without limits as to size, knowledge or power. He would have to be larger than creation or creation would be omnipresent. He would be larger than space which is the next thing to omnipresence.

Just as God's size, knowledge and power have no boundaries, neither are there any boundaries to His age for from everlasting to everlasting, thou art God (Psalms 90:2).

Such a Being is so absolute and unrelated to all other objects of thought that there exists nothing with which or with whom we may compare God. Hence, He is that single and solitary Being Whose goings forth have been from of old—from everlasting.

Of what substance does such an Omnipresent Being consist? Is God Matter or Material Substance? No! Jesus said that God is a Spirit—not that God has a Spirit as an attribute of His Being, but God is a Spirit. As a Spirit Substance, He is everywhere present at the same time. He is present in heaven and in earth without any separation of this substance from the heaven of the heavens to any place on earth.

Moreover, since God is unlimited as to size, God extends beyond all of creation into areas that are timeless and spaceless (if the word "spaceless" is sufficient to express a limitless God beyond the barriers of space and time).

As a Being of Spirit Substance in contrast to material substance, God is One Spirit not three. Although the scriptures speak of the seven spirits of God, the reference is either to seven angels, who are called ministering spirits, or to seven attributes of God's One Spirit (Isaiah 11:1-3).

It is totally impossible to have more than One Omnipresent, Omniscient, Omnipotent Being, otherwise the scriptures which tell us that there is One God, or that God is One, would be false. The gross effect would be Tritheism. While the effect of much of the so-called Trinitarian theory is a Tritheism of sorts, it does not go so far as to say grossly that there are three Beings of Omnipresence, Omniscience and Omnipotence. That is to say, the theory does deny three Gods; but some of the implications force a man of reason to wonder how such a denial can seriously be offered in the light of other statements. However, for the time, we will be content to respect the theory's denial of belief in three gods.

If there existed three distinct and separate omnisciences, omnipresences and omnipotences for each of the three alleged persons in the Deity, there would, of course, be three gods without argument. However, if the so-called persons of the Deity each have the same identical Spirit as their omnipresent substance, then the alleged three persons would be faces or fronts of this omnipresent substance called Spirit. We have seen, however, that person and persons are improper and inadequate terms to identify God, either in His absolute and basic Substance or in His Self Revelation.

The big question is: Is God so big as a Spirit Being that He is not only in space and time but also external to space and time due to His omnipresence and eternality?

It is the judgment of this writer that God is measureless as to size, knowledge, power and life, being absolutely infinite to the extreme implications of that word.

GOD IS NOT THREE PERSONS

IS GOD REALLY THREE PERSONS OR INDIVIDUALS?

In order to perpetuate the notion that there is a plurality of individuals in the Godhead, the terms "Three Persons" and "Trinity" have been added. Neither the term Three Persons nor Trinity can be found in the Bible; and, therefore, no one is obligated by the Bible to adhere to such language. There are better ways to describe God. These terms were extracted from Latin, not from the Hebrew, Chaldean, or Greek.

Whenever the term "three persons" is used concerning men, the mind automatically thinks of three separate individuals. When the same term is applied to describe the Godhead, one thinks of three individuals or three Gods, even if followed by a quick explanation that these three are really One God. This author holds no brief against the Latin language, but if a Latin word or any word alters the intent and meaning of the original scriptures, then other words must be found and used.

Why not simply say as both the Old and New Testaments do: "Hear, O Israel: The LORD our God is one LORD." "God is One" (Deuteronomy 6:4 and Galatians 3:20).

Then describe God as a Spirit (John 4:24) being bigger than the heaven of heavens (2 Chronicles 6:18). Wherever man might go, whether to heaven or hell, or to dwell in the uttermost parts of the sea, God (a Spirit) is there. Since there is only one Spirit (Ephesians 4:4), and God is a Spirit, then God is everywhere that man might go. This teaches that God is omnipresent. Paul said that in Him we "live, and move, and have our being" (Acts 17:28). He also said, "One God and Father of all, who is above all, and through all, and in you all" (Ephesians 4:6).

After showing God to be a Universal Spirit, show how that the Word was the means that God used to make the worlds, and that the Word was made flesh and was named Jesus Christ (John 1:1-3, 14). In short, the Spirit spoke through His Word-Image and the worlds were made. The Word-Image was then made flesh and was called Jesus Christ. The Word was called a Son only because He was born of Mary. The Word was God expressed in creation and became a Son by virtue of being brought forth in the form and manner as described in the Bible. You see, God made all things by Jesus Christ (Ephesians 3:9), but He existed in the form of the Word until through Mary He took human form.

The Word is thus made or manifested in the flesh (1 Timothy 3:16) and is the visible expression of the invisible God to the world in a visible body. In John we see: "Philip saith unto him, Lord, shew us the Father, and it sufficeth us. Jesus saith unto him, Have I been so long time with you, and yet hast thou not known me, Philip? he that hath seen me hath seen the Father; and how sayest thou then, Shew us the Father?" (John 14:8-9).

Then simply show that the Holy Ghost is a measure of God poured out upon flesh. You will recall that Jesus said that He would send the disciples another Comforter and referred to the Holy Ghost as He and Him. Then Jesus clearly showed that the Comforter was Jesus Himself in another form (Spirit form) when He said, "I will not leave you comfortless: I will come to you" (John 14:18). If Jesus Christ did not come into the believer in a Spirit or another form, He could not get into the human body. Paul told the Corinthian Church, "Know ye not your own selves, how that Jesus Christ is in you, except ye be reprobates?" (2 Corinthians 13:5).

Although the language God used concerning Himself may sound as though one being is talking to, or of another being, it is to distinguish the variety of forms or manifestations. In short, when Jesus spoke of the Holy Ghost as one might speak of a third individual, it was to differentiate as to the kind of self revelation or manifestation indicated.

Anyone who thinks twice about the matter will realize that each believer cannot have three persons dwelling in Him at the same time, and yet the Bible tells us the following:

"Your body is the temple of the Holy Ghost" (1 Corinthians 6:19).

The One God who is the Father of all is "in you all" (Ephesians 4:6).

Paul said that "Jesus Christ is in you" (2 Corinthians 13:5).

If each of us had the Holy Ghost in him (and we were filled with it), and the Father was in us, and Jesus Christ was in us, then *who* do we have in us? There would be three persons for each believer. There would not only be three persons in the Godhead, but each believer would be filled with three *persons*.

The variety and diversity of God's self revelation forces Him to use language that may seem to imply plurality of individuals, but if such is accepted literally the effect would be a belief in a plurality of Gods.

TRINITARIAN MISTAKE

WHAT IS IT THAT THE TRINITARIANS DO NOT UNDERSTAND ABOUT THE CHRISTIAN MONOTHEISTS POSITION?

The One God doctrine of the Christian Monotheist does not deny the Father, Son and Holy Ghost; but rejects such Tritheistic ideas expressed and implied by the adduction of such terms as: Three Separate and Distinct Persons in the Godhead as God the Father, God the Son, and God the Holy Ghost.

They apparently do not realize that true Christian Monotheism includes the total Godhead in its doctrine, but do not accept language that splits God into co-equals. This is Tritheism in a modified form but still Tritheism.

The Oneness view includes God in His Omnipresence, His particularity in Christ and His impartation to Believers, as the Holy Ghost. It does not omit a single element in the Deity, but places every aspect in a balanced perspective, without ending up with a plurality of Gods as the Tritheists do.

The Christian Monotheists have a statement on the Godhead that is far more accurate and informative than the double talk that had to be invented by Tritheists to make a plurality of gods palatable to the public. Instead of the

Godhead, a Three Headed God is implied and expressed.

Actually, if the full truth on this subject were known by the vast numbers of true Christians, and the Christian Monotheists views were presented correctly, many would believe and perhaps already basically believe now what is found in this book.

ETERNAL SON OF GOD?

IS IT POSSIBLE TO BE AN ETERNAL SON?

Is Jesus the eternal Son of God? Impossible! Did Jesus Christ eternally exist? Yes! A contradiction? No! Jesus was in existence from eternity as the Word in an image as well as in speech. He was in God's bosom as an image and as a plan or purpose. The beginning of the creation by God was when God uttered His idea in the nature of Speech with creation was the result. As in Revelation 3:14, Jesus is called the "beginning of the creation of God." This does not mean that Jesus Christ is God's first created Being, but that the Word-Image is first before creation. This Word later became flesh and was named Jesus Christ. Hence, the scripture: "God, who created all things by Jesus Christ" (Ephesians 3:9) is understood.

The beginning of creation was when God made heaven and earth by His Word (Genesis 1:1, John 1:1-3, Revelation 3:14). This Word became His Son through the virgin birth and this is not an abnormal title to identify any child born of a woman, provided the child is a male. "But when the fulness of the time was come, God sent forth his Son, made of a woman, made under the law" (Galatians 4:4). The Sonship of Jesus is stressed in two relations: His birth and His resurrection (Hebrews 1:6 and Acts 13:33).

Jesus is God projected into the world of flesh by means of the virgin birth. If Jesus had appeared without going through the process of birth, He would have been called the Angel of the Lord as in Exodus 3:1-14, inasmuch as His Word-Image was concealed behind an angel Theophany. It is the form and manner of His entrance into the world and out of the tomb that the idea of birth and sonship arises. Otherwise, He would be termed a Messenger or Angel of the LORD. This is not to say that Jesus was another angel in the Old Testament, but God did take angelic forms then.

Hence, when you read the words that Jesus is the Son of God, remember it is usually referring to the virgin birth. Say what you will, the Sonship of Jesus has its validity in the fact of His virgin birth; and he is an anti-christ who denies the virgin birth of Jesus Christ. This is where the Son of God issue arises primarily.

LOGICAL RESULTS OF TRINITARIANISM

WHAT IS THE RESULT OF TRINITARIAN THEORY WHEN CARRIED TO ITS LOGICAL CONCLUSION?

Well, if Father, Son and Holy Ghost are to be understood as Three Separate and Distinct Persons, then it can be proven that the man Christ Jesus had all Three Persons in Himself.

If the Eternal Son of God came down and was compressed into the form of a babe to be born with the seed of the woman, then Jesus Christ is the Eternal Son of God united with the Son of man. Then at His Baptism by John, the Third Person in the so-called Blessed Trinity came upon Him and He was full of the Holy Ghost (Luke 4:1). Somewhere along the way, the First Person in the Holy Trinity came into Jesus, for Jesus said, "The Father that dwelleth in me, he doeth the works" (John 14:10).

All three of these Separate and Distinct Persons would be found in the Lord Jesus Christ, if God is Three Persons.

By the same token, it can be proven that each True Christian has the Father in Him (Ephesians 4:6); has the Son (Jesus Christ) in Him (Galatians 1:16; 2 Corinthians 13:5); and has the Holy Ghost in him (1 Corinthians 6:19).

By separating the Deity into Persons, there are Three Separate and Distinct Persons that bear record in heaven—the Father, the Word and the Holy Ghost. Yet, Jesus said that He was with the Church always (Matthew 28:20). The Holy Ghost is to abide with us forever (John 14:16), and one would expect the Father to be as faithful to us as the other two! How can the Three be in heaven, and the Three be in each believer at the same time?

The Trinitarian would have to say that each Person would be in each Christian in the Spirit. Yes, but how many Spirits? Is the Spirit of the Father separate and distinct from the Spirit of the Son? If so, there would be Three Separate and Distinct Spirits for each of the Persons alleged to be in the Godhead. There is One Spirit (Ephesians 4:4).

TRINITARIAN CONFUSION

IS THE TRINITARIAN THEORY AS SIMPLE AND PRACTICAL AS THEY HAVE IMAGINED?

No. If the Second Person of the Godhead became man in the incarnation, and the Third Person filled Him after He was baptized by John the Baptist, and Jesus said that the Father dwelt in Him (which would be the First Person in Trinitarian theory), then in Jesus Christ dwelt the First, Second and Third Persons of this sublime Trinity. This would be in effect admitting, in a circuitous way, the view they condemn in what they are fond of calling the "Jesus Only" people.

They would have a time explaining how these Three are bearing record in heaven. The Three Person theory puts all of the Three in heaven as of now (1 John 5:7), yet the Holy Ghost is in the Church on earth (1 Corinthians 6:19); Jesus Christ is supposed to be in the Christian (2 Corinthians 13:5); and Paul said that the Father was "in you all" (Ephesians 4:6). This makes Three Persons in each Christian as well as Three Persons in heaven.

But, the Trinitarian will protest, this is God in His Omnipresence. Does each heavenly Person have His own

Omnipresence? If so, there is no escape from Tritheism (Three Gods). If The Omnipresence of the Three is the One Spirit, then the Father, Son and Holy Ghost in us is One, not Three. If Father, Son, and Holy Ghost are separate and distinct as Persons, do they cease to be Persons when viewed as being within the Christians? If so, what is a person? Do we have the Father, Son and Holy Ghost in us? Why would Jesus Christ bother to send another Comforter if He was coming to be with the Church? Why would He pray the Father to send another Comforter if the Father was yet coming to be "in you all"?

WHAT PURPOSE— TRINITARIANISM!

WHAT DOES THE TRINITARIAN THEORY ATTEMPT TO DO? WHAT PROBLEMS HAVE BEEN CREATED BY THE TRINITARIAN THEORY?

Trinitarianism is an attempt to compromise Tritheism (a belief in three Gods) with Monotheism (a belief in One God), resulting in a hybrid (or mixed) doctrine. The doctrine of Trinitarianism is neither true Monotheism nor exact Tritheism (but is an attempted accommodation for both.

The Christian "One God" believer cannot accept Trinitarianism nor can the Tritheist fully accept it. There are millions of people who feel so unable to fathom the mystery, that whatever the people say (who are supposed to know) is accepted without argument. In short, just as laymen are prone to leave the deep things of the law to the judges and lawyers, religious people leave matters of deep theology to the theologians.

To the undiscerning it seems logical to say that the Son and the Father must be two different persons, for whoever heard of a son and his father being the same one? And this is true, but God is not a person in the same category that people are persons! The term *person* is inappropriate in His case. The word *Person* is used of God in Hebrews 1:3, but all good scholars agree that the word *substance* is the better rendition from the Greek.

Also the birth of Jesus is so uniquely different from the birth of all other children. He was without an earthly father. He existed before His birth. The Holy Ghost is His Father as far as the Virgin Mary is concerned. He is said to be from everlasting, and only God is from everlasting. If He was an Eternal Son, then Jesus Christ consisted of four persons—The Father, the Holy Ghost, the Eternal Son, Who dwelt in the Son of man.

The fallacy rests upon the superimposed terms of "Persons Who are Separate and Distinct." If there are Three Persons Who are Separate and Distinct, in the Incarnation the Eternal Son came in the Son of Man. Then at His Baptism by John the Holy Ghost came upon Him (Luke 3:16, 17; 4:1); and somewhere, either at the baptism, at His birth or sometime afterward the Father dwelt in Him (John 14:10).

The Father dwelt in Him, the Son dwelt in Him and the Holy Ghost dwelt in Him. Three Separate and Distinct Persons had to dwell in Him, and He as man would be the fourth person. The scriptures declare the Father, Son and

Holy Ghost are in Jesus.

If He were an Eternal Son and was God, He would be fully capable of being born without His Father. Some Trinitarians say Jesus was Omnipresent, Omniscient and Omnipotent before His birth. The Eternal Son could be the Father of the only begotten Son, since the Eternal Son left most of Himself behind when He came in Mary. Actually, the term person or persons is not adequate, and when pursued falls apart as illogical. It is totally impossible, either in scripture or in reason.

How big do you think the Eternal Son had to be to impart into the Virgin with Himself. From this unity the child grew and was born in due time.

If the Son before conception is as vast and eternal as some Tritheists say, very little of God, the Son, ever was conceived by Mary.

The fact is that such names as God, LORD, Almighty and Jehovah are identifying and descriptive terms to indicate something about the nature of the Supreme Being. When the Supreme Being adopted human nature with His Divine and Eternal Nature through the virgin birth, a whole host of relational terms were attached to describe the Mystery in a way that man might analogically gain some knowledge of God.

God is One Everlasting Spirit Who caused the existence of all created things by willing and expressing them to be so. This Expression of Himself in creation is called the Word. The Word is the One God expressed in creation.

God's expression in this Creation was meant to reveal the Invisible God Who expressed Himself. It is this Word or Self Revelation that was made flesh and called the only begotten of the Father (John 1:14).

The Son of God is that composite of God and man in unity as distinguished from the same God exterior to that fusion. God in this Theophany is the same God that is called the Father or God in His Omnipresence. The Father is the Omnipresence, Omniscience and Omnipotence of the Son. The Son is the Particular Tabernacle wherein the Shekinah Glory that used to dwell in the Tabernacle of Moses indwelt. Hence, we see the Father, and come to the Father, through Jesus, as Israel did through the Tabernacle. Jesus is Priest, Sacrifice, Altar, Veil, Holy of Holies, and all and in all.

Trinitarianism is based upon a superficial understanding of the Bible, through human reasoning superimposed upon the scriptures. Those who have adopted that view only go along because it has been accepted for so long and by so many. No person can actually examine the foundations of Trinitarianism with objectivity and not be shaken by the implications of this watered-down version of Tritheism.

ONE THRONE

ARE THERE TWO THRONES—ONE FOR THE FATHER AND THE OTHER FOR THE SON?

Is it not peculiar that when anyone gets a glimpse into heaven there is One throne and One sitting upon that throne? Those who in their minds create the picture of the Father sitting on His throne and His Son at His right side, are in for a shock when this pretty picture is eliminated by the book of Revelation:

"And immediately I was in the spirit: and, behold, a throne was set in heaven, and one sat on the throne" (Revelation 4:2).

"And I saw in the right hand of him that sat upon the throne" (Revelation 5:1).

Revelation 4:9-11 records that He that sat upon the one throne had created all things. In Revelation 5 a Lamb took the book out of His right hand. This has been construed to mean that the second *person* in the holy trinity took the book out of God's hand. However, read more carefully what is said: "And one of the elders saith unto me, Weep not: behold, the Lion of the tribe of Juda, the Root of David, hath prevailed to open the book, and to loose the seven seals thereof. And I beheld, and, lo, in the midst of the throne and of the four beasts, and in the midst of the elders, stood a Lamb as it had been slain, having seven horns and seven eyes, which are the seven Spirits of God sent forth into all the earth. And he came and took the book out of the right hand of him that sat upon the throne" (Revelation 5:5-7).

The Lion is the symbol of a King, and Jesus is the King of the Jews. He is a descendant of David after the flesh. He is the Lamb slain from the foundation of the world. This symbol represents Son in His sacrificial office, not as God. Jesus Christ is God's Son in relation to His virgin birth, and is David's Son according to the flesh (Romans 1:3). Hence, what we have here is the distinction made between Jesus Christ acting in His Office of Mediator, from that of His Deity.

That is to say, Jesus is presented here not as a second person or as God the Son, but as the Root of David—as the Lamb of God. Jesus does not actually have four legs, seven horns, seven eyes and wool. This is Jesus Christ being identified, symbolically, as the Lamb offering.

In another scene in the book of Revelation, Jesus Christ is God on this throne. I think you will all agree that Jesus said, "I am Alpha and Omega, the beginning and the ending, saith the Lord, which is, and which was, and which is to come, the Almighty"(Revelation 1:8).

In Revelation 21:5-7 this One who sat upon the throne said that He was Alpha and Omega: "And he that sat upon the throne said, Behold, I make all things new. And he said unto me, Write: for these words are true and faithful. And he said unto me, It is done. I am Alpha and Omega, the beginning and the end. I will give unto him that is athirst of the fountain of the water of life freely. He that overcometh shall inherit all things; and I will be his God, and he shall be my son."

There is only one throne and only One on the throne. But how did the Lamb (Jesus) in Revelation 5 become the God on the throne in Revelation 21? In Revelation 5 Jesus is revealed as man and mediator between God and men. He is not emphasized as man in Revelation 21, and instead His Deity is exposed to view. "There is One God and One Mediator between God and men, the man Christ Jesus" (1 Timothy 2:5).

In His Mediatorial Office Jesus is man, and in His Divinity He is God. In short, Jesus is God and He is man. He is "truly" God and He is "fully" man.

HOW BIG IS GOD?

HOW BIG IS GOD OUTSIDE OF JESUS' BODY?

The answer to this is already given in respect to His unlimited size as an Omnipresent Spirit Substance. To show His size, Isaiah said, "Thus saith the Lord, The heaven is my throne, and the earth is my footstool" (Isaiah 66:1). The throne is heaven and the earth is the footstool. There is not, in this instance, a throne in heaven, but heaven is the throne. In Revelation 4:5 God is particularized in a form. The form is symbolical in that "He that sat was to look upon like a jasper and a sardine stone" (Revelation 4:3).

And while a simple idea that the Father's Son is sitting on His right side is easier to imagine, yet the size of Deity, outside of the body of Jesus, is too large to picture on two small thrones with two man-sized individuals perched thereon.

At the right hand of God is simply a way of saying that the Lord Jesus Christ has been exalted to have all authority in heaven and in earth, and as Mediator between God and Men, He as man is the only avenue to God for salvation. It is only when we search for the reality behind the words used, that understanding can be obtained.

GOD'S IMAGE

DOES GOD HAVE AN IMAGE?

Yes, indeed. There is no evidence that God in His Omnipresence has an image, shape or form. However, ideally, God had what might be termed a "blue print" or an "outline image." It was in this image that God made man. It does not appear, however, that God made woman in His image or after this pattern. This image is the Word-Image.

Angels appear to be made after the general pattern of this image because they appeared as men to Abraham, Lot, Jacob and others. Although their substance is spirit while Adam's was matter, the general outline is approximately the same for angels and men.

The exact image is not fully disclosed. God would not let men see Him exactly as He would be if this outline were perfectly filled in. One might call this image the expressed Form or Shape as one of the attributes of the Omnipresent Spirit.

The Word-Image is this pattern, used for both angels and man. The angel of the LORD that is so often referred to in the Old Testament is more or less a rough outline that covered God's image.

God is not basically an angel but does basically also have a Shape (John 5:37). These manifestations in angel form were temporary, but had a typical or prophetical import. We have no reason to hold that God's appearances in any form in Old Testament times were permanent but was in some way related to the ideal Image or Form into which the Word-Image would emerge in the Incarnation.

For this reason, Jesus in His Divine Nature is the Word-Image encased in flesh. The flesh is the created image of man assumed through Mary. Hence, the form of God assumed the form of man—the uncreated image blended with, but was not obliterated by, the created image of man.

On the Mount of Transfiguration, the disciples saw the image of God radiating out, over and above the image of man before their eyes. This is a preview of the post resurrection—the shining out of the Divine Form. Just as the Divine Image is not obliterated by the incarnation but rather concealed, so in the resurrection the image of Jesus the man is not obliterated but rather lifted, blended into and put in focus to the Divine Image.

However, either image could be emphasized because Jesus related Himself to us in both ways. After His resurrection, Jesus showed that He was material (that had been changed) in that He could be handled, could eat and could be touched; but He also showed that He was spirit when He became invisible and passed through doors without them being opened. We do not know how this could be. Jesus bore the earthly image and He bore the heavenly Image.

We know what it is to bear the image of the earthly (1 Corinthians 15:49). Someday we shall also bear the image of the heavenly (1 Corinthians 15:59).

There is a natural body and there is a spiritual body (1 Corinthians 15:44).

In Jesus Christ the natural is not destroyed, but it certainly is immortalized in life, honor, glory and power. The earthly image is brought into focus with the heavenly image in Jesus Christ, the "God-Man."*

*God-Man is a term herein used to abbreviate the fact that Jesus had two natures in His being.

GENESIS 1:27

IS THERE A COMPLETELY SATISFACTORY ANSWER GIVEN TO GENESIS 1:26?

If a person is of a Tritheistic mind, the answer in Genesis 1:27 will not be accepted. To a Monotheist the answer of Genesis 1:27 is the basic answer.

"And God said, Let us make man in our image, after our likeness: and let them have dominion over the fish of the sea and over the fowl of the air, and over the cattle, and over all the earth, and over every creeping thing that creepeth upon the earth" (Genesis 1:26).

"So God created man in His own image, in the image of God created he him; male and female created he them" (Genesis 1:27).

Us and Our are omitted in this verse, and God created man in *His* own image, in the image of God created *He* him.

It is said that the Jews hold that God was talking to certain of His angels in Genesis 1:26. It was the Seraphims that the LORD asked "Who will go for us" in Isaiah 6:1-3, 8. It was Cherubims that God placed at the east of the garden of Eden, and a flaming sword, after God said: "Behold man is become as one of us" (Genesis 3:22, 24).

The similarity of men and angels is close when angels appear to men in nonsymbolical or non-visionary ways (Hebrews 2:7; Acts 1:10; Genesis 18:33; 19:1, etc.)

This is not said to imply that Angels actually performed the work of creating us or creating Adam, except in some auxiliary way. Malachi asked, "Hath not One God created us?" (Malachi 2:10). Jesus also said that it was *He* not *Them* that made male and female in the beginning: "Have ye not read, that he which made them at the beginning made them male and female?" (Matthew 19:4).

God's own Image is the Shape of the Father, also called the Form of God (John 5:37; Philippians 2:6-8).

ALPHA AND OMEGA

IS ALPHA AND OMEGA CALLED THE ALMIGHTY?

"I am Alpha and Omega, the beginning and the ending, saith the Lord, which is, and which was, and which is to come, the Almighty" (Revelation 1:8).

Alpha and Omega was identified as the one whom John saw on the isle called Patmos—Jesus Christ (Revelation 1:10-18).

Adam Clarke, in his commentary, found elsewhere in this book statements confirming that there cannot be two Almighties. If this is true, and it is true, then the One on the throne in Revelation 4 is the Alpha and Omega of Revelation 1; for the four beasts say of and to the One on the throne: "Holy, holy, holy, Lord God Almighty, which was, and is, and is to come" (Revelation 4:8).

And to clinch it, Revelation 21:5-7 identifies the One on this one throne as Alpha and Omega, and Alpha and Omega promised that He would be the God to the overcomer, and the overcomer would be His son:

"And he that sat upon the throne said, Behold, I make

all things new. And He said unto me, Write: for these words are true and faithful. And He said unto me, It is done. I am Alpha and Omega, the beginning and the end. I will give unto him that is athirst of the fountain of the water of life freely. He that overcometh shall inherit all things; and I will be his God, and he shall be my son."

Alpha and Omega are the first and last letters of the Greek alphabet. Words are made from a combination of letters. Jesus is the Word or the beginning and ending of God's self-revelation to man in time.

BEGINNING AND ENDING

IF GOD IS FROM EVERLASTING TO EVERLASTING AND HAS NO BEGINNING OR ENDING, WHY IS GOD SAID TO BE THE BEGINNING AND THE END?

Since beginning is a term related to the starting of something, and ending is a term related to the stopping of something, the obvious answer is: The beginning and the end has to do with God related to time and creation. He Who is essentially timeless and spaceless has, nevertheless, identified Himself to time and space through creation as the Word.

Hence, God in time and space is Creator; and, by virtue of the incarnation, is Redeemer. This is why Jesus Christ is called the Word made flesh—He is God as revealed in Creation incarnated into man.

Perhaps an illustration will help:

Imagine an unending canal of water. Place somewhere in this infinite stream or canal, locks or water walls (upper and lower locks). The canal is above the upper locks and is also below the lower locks. Identify the upper lock as the beginning and the lower lock as the ending. The everlasting God is an unending Spirit before the beginning and is an unending Spirit after the ending, but between the beginning and ending (illustrated by the upper and lower locks), is a part of that unending God in time and space. This aspect of God is called the Word or Self-Revelation part of the invisible and limitless God. "In the beginning was the Word, and the Word was with God, and the Word was God" (John 1:1).

The Word is God self-revealed in time and space due to creation, but the Word is not a separate Being from God—anymore than the water between the upper and lower locks of the canal is another water than from the stream above and below each lock.

This Word was further centralized and crystalized when the Word-Image was embodied, as to essential qualities, in the flesh or in a body (Jesus Christ). This crystalization or concentration of the God of creation in a body does not eliminate or reduce God's size so that less Deity existed in the universe, but rather the great universal Spirit (the Divine Substance) concentrated into an image or form—the Impressed Character of God's Substance or Nature, or the Image of God superimposed into the form of man. Hence, all the fulness of Divine Qualities including Image dwelleth in Him bodily (Colossians 2:9).

JESUS AS MAN AND GOD

IS JESUS CHRIST MORE THAN GOD? YES, BECAUSE HE IS MAN. IS JESUS CHRIST MORE THAN MAN? YES, BECAUSE HE IS GOD.

What name, symbol or term would one use to identify a Being Who is different from God and different from man, and yet is both? Since this composite Being is of both Divine and Human essence and is an offspring of each substance, He is called Son of God and Son of Man.

When called God, one is speaking of His Divine Substance; but to call Him man, one is speaking of His human substance. From His Divine Source, He is an offspring of the Spirit. From His human source, He is an offspring of the flesh.

John's task is to reveal Jesus from His Divine Origin; and, therefore, Son of God is the description given.

It is Luke's task to reveal Jesus from His human origin. Hence, Son of Man is the description given of Him.

Since God is One and God cannot create God, the God Substance in Jesus is God Himself. Jesus said, "I and my Father are one" (John 10:30). This is called a Theophany or "God in a body."

Jesus is more than God because He is also man; yet because He is less than *all of God,* He is less than God from the standpoint of quantity.

This sounds paradoxical but a brief explanation will help.

The Qualitative essence or substance of God's Divine nature is in Jesus Christ. In fact, the fulness of God's Qualitative Essence, as manifest from the beginning to the end, is in Jesus Christ, bodily. Quantitatively, God has no such boundaries, being infinite in every sense.

For this reason, the Father was in Jesus Christ, yet Jesus said that He was in the Father. Hence, in time and body God was in Christ (John 14:9, 2 Corinthians 5:19); but this God Incarnate Form was in the Father who fills space, time, and even beyond Fatherhood into eternity.

To call Jesus only man and not also Son of Man, would deny the humanity of all humanity from whence He proceeded. To call Jesus, God, and not also Son of God would deny the Divinity of the rest of God in infinity, in Omnipresence, in Omnipotence and in Omniscience.

Unlike humanity, who are many (Jesus is of human origin), God is single and solitary in His everlasting substance and not plural. When God projected Himself into this humanity of Jesus, it was nothing other than "God was manifest in the flesh" (1 Timothy 3:16).

As man, Jesus was representative for men; but as God, Jesus is one with the Father, for God is One. "A mediator is not a mediator of one, but God is one" (Galatians 3:20). "There is one God and one mediator between God and men, the man Christ Jesus" (1 Timothy 2:5).

Perhaps an imperfect analogy may be drawn: Let the water be likened unto God, Who is a Spirit; and let an iceberg be likened unto Jesus Christ. The water is in the iceberg and the iceberg is in the water. Ice is water in solid form. Jesus Christ is God in man form. This allows us to say that water is ice and ice is water. By the same token, we can say God is Jesus Christ and Jesus Christ is God. There are the liquid and solid manifestations of water. There is the Omnipresent invisible Spirit and the particular visible Jesus Christ—One God in general, as well as in a particular body.

SON OF GOD, SON OF MAN?

WHY IS JESUS CALLED SON OF GOD AND SON OF MAN? WHY IS THE BOOK OF ST. JOHN WRITTEN?

"But these are written, that ye might believe that Jesus is the Christ, the Son of God; and that believing ye might have life (ZOE—everlasting life) through his name" (John 20:31).

How did John think he could cause people to believe that they could obtain everlasting life through believing that Jesus is the Christ, the Son of God; and that by believing they might have that kind of life through His name? By showing that Jesus originated from a Divine Source and was the creative life force of God in the beginning of the creation of God.

"In the beginning was the Word, and the Word was with God, and the Word was God. The same was in the beginning with God. All things were made by him; and without him was not anything made that was made. In him was life [ZOE]; and the life [ZOE] was the light of men" (John 1:1-4).

Was the *Word* called Son of God before His birth of Mary? No. He was called the "Word." When is the Word called the Son or the only begotten of the Father? "And the Word was made flesh, and dwelt among us, (and we beheld his glory, the glory as of the only begotten of the Father), full of grace and truth" (John 1:14).

What was the effect of this connection of the Word with the flesh? The connection of the Word with the flesh was the alloying of divine life with human life. Hence, the only begotten of the Father was Mary's firstborn, and from her side He was man while from the Divine side He was God.

If there is only One God, and the Son of God is God, did God produce God or did God generate God—thus resulting in two Gods? No, this is not the effect of Jesus' birth. Since Jesus is two natures in one body and not one nature, He is more than God in that He is man also; and He is more than man in that He is God.

The term to call a God-Man, who is such due to a birth and due to the two sources from whence He came, is "Son of God" (springing from a Divine Source) and "Son of Man" (springing from a human source). John writes a gospel in which His divine origin is emphasized and the big term is Son of God. Luke's gospel emphasizes His human origin and the big term is Son of Man.

SEPARATE PERSON?

ISN'T JESUS A SEPARATE PERSON FROM HIS FATHER JUST AS HE IS A SEPARATE PERSON FROM HIS MOTHER?

No. The error here rests on the use of the word "person." The term person is inappropriate since God should not be classified as humans are. There is only *One* God but *many* people. Jesus is man, but He is a separate person from all men, as the term person is used in connection with people. In reference to God, Jesus is not separate from God, except God in the flesh which distinguishes Him from the rest of God exterior to the flesh.

Before "God was manifest in the flesh" (1 Timothy 3:16), He was known in relation to creation as the Word. "In the beginning was the Word" (John 1:1). "In the beginning God created heaven and earth" (Genesis 1:1).

The Word was not a separate Being from God, for "the Word was God" (John 1:1).

Why was the *Word with God* if the Word was God?

Well, you see, before there was a creation there was no beginning—only everlasting. "Before the mountains were brought forth, or ever thou hadst formed the earth and the world, even from everlasting to everlasting, thou art God" (Psalms 90:2).

When God made heaven and earth after His Word-Image entered into Time, in an act of creation, the word "beginning" was introduced. This shows that heaven and earth are not from everlasting. However, God Who is from everlasting is now linked to Time and Creation by an Act of Speech through His Word-Image.

By what term can God join Himself to a beginning and to heaven and earth and still be known as without a beginning and apart from His creation?

John 1:1 uses the term *Word* to link God to Time (Beginning) and creation. This separates God in His infinity from the finite—His Absoluteness from His Relatedness. In order that the believer may connect God's Relatedness to His Absoluteness, John also says, "the Word was God."

Thus, the One God of eternity related Himself to time; and the One Uncreated God related Himself to creation. By this method, He is in and related to all of Time and Creation, whether invisible or visible, whether animate or inanimate.

It may at first leave an impression of a duality of God, when, actually, it is a mode of self-revelation.

Now the God of Time and Creation is the same God separate from Time and Creation.

However, a question may be asked: If the Word is God in time and creation, when time is no longer, will the Word cease, too?

To forestall this impression, John said of the Word, "In him was life [ZOE—everlasting life]; and the life was the light of men" (John 1:4).

Is this why John went all the way back to the beginning—to show that Jesus Christ was God in creation before He was made flesh, in order to show that He Who was in the flesh was fully capable of transferring life to all who believed on Him? Yes.

Thus, God bridges the difficulty by calling that expression of Himself exercised in creating heaven and earth "The Word," and it was "The Word" that came in the flesh.

Now the problem is: How can God be united to man and in this unity of natures be known in such a sense that He is not bound nor limited to or by this fusion? The problem is different from the beginning of creation in that the Word entered into Time. Now the same Word is to be born.

What will God call Himself in such a birth? He called Himself the Word to connect Himself to the beginning of time and creation, but what will God call Himself in this virgin birth?

God distinguished Himself in relation to Time and Creation by the term "The Word," from His apartness from Time and Creation. Now, in God's involvement in the flesh, He denominates Himself as Son of God, whereas in creation He denominated Himself as "The Word."

Why call Himself Son of God if the Son of God is God? In order to distinguish God apart from the flesh, as well as incarnated in the flesh. This permits us to see the One God in different aspects:

As Everlasting God, He is outside of time and creation. As "the Word" God is inside time and creation. As "Son of God," God is in the flesh and is called Jesus. The God outside of creation is the same God Who is in creation, and the God Who is in creation is the same God that was in Christ reconciling the world unto Himself (2 Corinthians 5:19).

GOD'S VOICE

IF JESUS IS GOD'S WORD-IMAGE IN A BODY, CAN GOD SPEAK OUTSIDE OF THIS BODY?

Certainly. When Jesus was anointed with the Holy Ghost (Acts 10:38), after His baptism by John the Baptist, God spoke from heaven declaring, "This is my beloved Son, in whom I am well pleased" (Matthew 3:17). Christ means "Anointed One."

On the day of Pentecost, God spoke out of the lips of about one hundred and twenty persons at one time (Acts 1; 2:1-14). There is no limit self-imposed upon God in relation to the place or places He may speak from. However, God has specifically told us, "This is my beloved Son, in whom I am well pleased; *hear ye him*" (Matthew 17:5).

All that God may say will be related to the scope of the Word Incarnate, for the Word is Alpha and Omega—The Almighty revealed in the flesh.

JESUS CREATOR

ISN'T JESUS CALLED THE CREATOR?

Yes, indeed He is. But as Creator, the reader must discern between Jesus as Creator and as creature. He is "the beginning of the creation of God." This has clear reference to Jesus as the Word-Image through Whom all creation was made. In the beginning He is Creator (John 1:1-3). In the virgin birth He is Creator fused with created. Hence, the distinction: In His Deity Jesus was never created, either in the beginning nor later; but when Deity and Humanity met in the virgin born Son, Creator and created are joined—God and man were united in the Lord Jesus Christ.

St. John is a book exclusively "Written, that ye might believe that Jesus is the Christ (Messiah, Anointed One), the Son of God; and that believing ye might have life through his name" (John 20:31). This Life is from the Greek word ZOE and means Eternal Life.

In this Word "Was life; and the life was the light of men" (John 1:4).

This injection of life, God's life, into the seed of the woman related two natures together—there emerged Divine Life (Zoe) and human life (psyche or soul) and biological physical life in the virgin birth.

"For the life [Zoe] was manifested, and we have seen it, and bear witness, and shew unto you that eternal life, which was with the Father, and was manifested unto us" (1 John 1:2).

This Eternal life is in the Divine Nature of Jesus Christ.

GOD THE SON?

ISN'T JESUS CALLED "GOD THE SON"?

No. This is a term added by the pluralists. Neither is

the Holy Spirit called "God the Holy Ghost." The scripture implied by the question is Hebrews 1:8, 9: "But unto the Son he saith, Thy throne, O God, is for ever and ever: a sceptre of righteousness is the sceptre of thy kingdom. Thou hast loved righteousness, and hated iniquity; therefore God, even thy God, hath anointed thee with the oil of gladness above thy fellows."

The reader must recognize the condition existing in the Hebrew Christian Church, to whom the writer addressed his epistle. These Christians were drifting away from the New Testament economy (Hebrews 2:1-4), and somehow had rated Jesus Christ either equal or lower than angels.

The writer admitted that Jesus was made lower than the angels, but that this was for the suffering of death "That he by the grace of God should taste death for every man" (Hebrews 2:9).

But the writer showed that this virgin born Son is more than angels and men, in that He is God (Hebrews 1:3-8).

Even as a man, He was above His fellows: "Thou hast loved righteousness, and hated iniquity; therefore God, even thy God, hath anointed thee with the oil of gladness above thy fellows."

Jesus was anointed above any king or priest—whether Aaron, David or any other. Christ or Messiah means the "Anointed One." (Read Matthew 3:17 and Acts 10:38.)

The point of the Hebrew epistle is to show how much better and greater Jesus is than angels and men in that He is God to the angels, and as to men, He is "Anointed" above His fellows.

Why did the scripture say, "Unto the Son He saith, Thy throne, O God?" The answer is: The writer is saying that this Son is actually God in the flesh. He is God's bright glory. He is the Impressed Character of God's Substance. Look deeper ye potential apostates—this Son is actually God if you will turn the coin over and look on the other side. Are ye so blind that you look no deeper than the outer veil?

What about the text: "Sit on my right hand, until I make thine enemies thy footstool?" (Hebrews 1:13).

This right hand of God is symbolical of power and favor to which the one Who was made a little lower than the angels is now exalted above the angels.

You see, this one on the right hand is there because "when he had by himself purged our sins (on the cross), sat down on the right hand of the Majesty on high" (Hebrews 1:3). Only man can die. God cannot die. How can eternal life die? In every instance when Jesus is said to now be on God's right hand, it is a follow up to His death. Hence, it is the God in His human nature that died and is seated on the right hand (Hebrews 5:5-8; 8:1; 10:12, 13; Acts 2:29-36).

"On the right hand" is Christ in His kingly, priestly and mediatorial office.

Our High Priest was tempted (Hebrews 4:15). God cannot be tempted (James 1:13).

Every high priest is taken from among men (Hebrews 5:1, 5-8).

It is as King-Priest after the order of Melchizedek that Jesus is on the right hand. There is only one throne in heaven (Revelation 4).

Jesus was to sit on David's throne as the seed of David according to the flesh (Acts 2:30). More than David, Jesus is a priest; but more than a King and Priest, Jesus was a prophet like unto Moses. In summary, at the right hand Jesus is a priest. He is a king with all authority in heaven and earth after the order of David over the earth in a greatly magnified sense, and as Melchizedek in His permanent priesthood after the resurrection from the dead. At the right hand is a summary way of saying that Jesus is the perfection of all men who were anointed from Adam to John the Baptist—anointed above thy fellows. The total anointing was placed upon Jesus. Every part of the Spirit that anointed holy men of God was combined and anointed to Jesus—"God giveth not the Spirit by measure unto him" (John 3:34).

"Therefore being by the right hand of God exalted, and having received of the Father the promise of the Holy Ghost, he hath shed forth this, which ye now see and hear" (Acts 2:33).

David did not ascend up to heaven to be seated as supreme human potentate, but his Son after the flesh did.

Whatever typical men of the Old Testament were, they pre-figured Christ in various degrees and ways. Hence, Jesus is all they foreshadowed, and then some. For while He is Master and Husband, as the Hebrew word Adonai implies, He is also LORD—LORD OF LORDS (Revelation 19:16). He is not only Adonai on the right hand; but if one will look deeper into His actual Deity, He is JEHOVAH Himself in a body.

At the right hand of God is not to be taken literally. The scripture tells us that Jesus was to sit on God's right hand until His enemies were made His footstool. If He was to sit until the last enemy was subdued, He would still be sitting. However, Jesus is pictured in Stephen's vision as *standing* on the right hand of God (Acts 7:56). If Jesus was told to sit, then why is He standing? He was told to sit until His enemies were made His footstool!

FATHER AND LORD

WHY IS JESUS NOT CALLED GOD IN RELATION TO THE FATHER?

"From God our Father, and the Lord Jesus Christ" (Romans 1:7).

"From God our Father, and from the Lord Jesus Christ" (1 Corinthians 1:3).

"From God our Father, and from the Lord Jesus Christ" (2 Corinthians 1:2).

"Blessed be God, even the Father of our Lord Jesus Christ, the Father of mercies" (2 Corinthians 1:3).

"From God the Father, and from our Lord Jesus Christ" (Galatians 1:3).

"Blessed be the God and Father of our Lord Jesus Christ" (Ephesians 1:3).

"That the God of our Lord Jesus Christ" (Ephesians 1:17).

"One God and Father of all" (Ephesians 4:6).

"From God the Father and the Lord Jesus Christ" (Ephesians 6:23).

"But to us there is but one God, the Father" (1 Corinthians 8:6).

There are other scriptures in which the same is found:

Philippians 1:2; Colossians 1:2; 3:17; 1 Thessalonians 1:1; Philippians 2:11; 1 Thessalonians 3:13; 2 Thessalonians 1:1-2; 2 Thessalonians 2:16; 1 Timothy 1:1, 2; 2 Timothy 1:2; Titus 1:4; Philemon 3; James 1:1; 1 Peter 1:3, 2 Peter 1:1, 2; 2 John 3; Jude 1; Revelation 1:1.

and

"But to us there is but one God, the Father, of whom are all things, and we in him; and one Lord Jesus Christ, by whom are all things, and we by him" (1 Corinthians 8:6).

"God, who created all things *by* Jesus Christ" (Ephesians 3:9).

"For *by* him were all things created that are in heaven, and that are in earth. . .all things were created *by* him: . . .*by* Him all things consist" (Colossians 1:16, 17).

God is an Omnipresent Spirit. He is the source or Father of Whom are all things. God's Word is, of course, Himself Expressed and is the means whereby He created heaven and earth, with all things therein.

This Word was made flesh and named Jesus Christ—God was manifest in the flesh. When the Deity is primarily in mind, and the phrase "God our Father" is employed; and if related to the fleshly manifestation of the WORD in the same verse, the Lordship in contradistinction to Fatherhood is carefully pointed out. Jesus in the flesh is the Lordship emphasized from the human side, but at times also from the divine side. Father is a paternal title and Lord is a ruler title.

Hence, the Son is not called God when the Paternal and Lordship sides are distinguished. Jesus said that the Father was the Only True God (John 17:3). Therefore when Jesus is called God it is identifying Himself as the same one called the Father in other places. There is no such thing as God the son etc.

LORD and Lord

WHAT DO THE MANY SCRIPTURES MEAN BY SAYING "GOD OUR FATHER AND THE (or OUR) LORD JESUS CHRIST" IF TWO ARE NOT INTENDED?

Psalms 110:1 introduces LORD and Lord in a relationship that seems to indicate a Lord other than the LORD. From the general tenor of the scriptures it appears that LORD is a Name and Lord is an office held in relation to humankind.

"Therefore let all the house of Israel know assuredly, that God hath made that same Jesus whom ye have crucified, both Lord and Christ" (Acts 2:36).

Jesus indicates that His Authority in heaven and earth had been given to Him, "And Jesus came and spake unto them, saying, All power [authority] is given unto me in heaven and in earth" (Matthew 28:18).

He also said in His prayer to the Father, "As thou hast given him power over all flesh, that he should give eternal life to as many as thou hast given him" (John 17:2).

The One Paul called, the Lord, died and was raised from the dead, so we are dealing with some one capable of dying. Now it should be clear that God cannot die, therefore, the Lord is David's Son—the Son of David after the flesh. It is this same Jesus Christ Who is said to be at the right hand of God.

However, from other scriptures there is more to Jesus than humanity, for the second Adam is the LORD from heaven. Did the LORD from heaven derive His LORDSHIP or Authority? Of course not, for this is the other side of Jesus that is a mystery—for this is Jehovah or LORD (Jeremiah 23:5, 6). For LORD and Lord were united in Jesus Christ.

God has intended that man shall have dominion over the works of His hands. If you will read closely you will see in Peter's message on the day of Pentecost that it was David's Son who was to be resurrected and seated on His throne at the right hand of God:

"Men and brethren, let me freely speak unto you of the patriarch David, that he is both dead and buried, and his sepulchre is with us unto this day.

"Therefore being a prophet, and knowing that God had sworn with an oath to him, that of the fruit of his loins, according to the flesh, he would raise up Christ to sit on his throne;

"He seeing this before spake of the resurrection of Christ, that his soul was not left in hell, neither his flesh did see corruption.

"This Jesus hath God raised up, whereof we all are witnesses.

"Therefore being by the right hand of God exalted, and having received of the Father the promise of the Holy Ghost, he hath shed forth this, which ye now see and hear.

"For David is not ascended into the heavens: but he saith himself, The Lord said unto my Lord, Sit thou on my right hand, Until I make thy foes thy footstool.

"Therefore let all the house of Israel know assuredly, that God hath made that same Jesus, whom ye have crucified, both Lord and Christ" (Acts 2:29-36).

Even from the beginning God had ordained that man should have Lordship or dominion over the works of His hands (Genesis 1:26, 28). Of course, the overall Lordship is God in His Deity. This is indicated by Jesus' words, "I thank thee, O Father, Lord of heaven and earth" (Matthew 11:25).

That Lordship was ordained to man and not to angels, is indicated by the writer to the Hebrews: "For unto the angels hath he not put in subjection the world to come, whereof we speak."

"But one in a certain place testified, saying, What is man, that thou art mindful of him? or the son of man, that thou visitest him?

"Thou madest him a little lower than the angels; thou crownedst him with glory and honour, and didst set him over the works of thy hands:

"Thou hast put all things in subjection under his feet. For in that he put all in subjection under him, he left nothing that is not put under him. But now we see not yet all things put under him.

"But we see Jesus, who was made a little lower than the angels for the suffering of death, crowned with glory and honour" (Hebrews 2:5-9).

The discerning reader of the Bible must carefully recognize that when Jesus Christ is called Lord in context with God our Father, that the reference to His Lordship is not to Him as Jehovah but Adonai. This word Lord sometimes refers to God and sometimes to man. It means Master or Husband. This Jesus is, to His Disciples and Church.

Jesus in His Deity is called Lord in Hebrews 1: "And Thou Lord, in the beginning hast laid the foundation of the earth; and the heavens are the works of thine hands" (verse 10).

Except when quoting Psalms 110:1, the New Testament writers did not distinguish Yahweh from Adonai as far as spelling YAHWEH as LORD and ADONAI as Lord. They used one Greek word "Kurios" for both words, and is simply translated Lord. This makes it difficult to discern whether Jesus is fulfilling His Lordship as David's Lord or as David's LORD (Jehovah).

THE ONLY TRUE GOD

DID JESUS SAY THAT THE FATHER WAS THE ONLY TRUE GOD?

Yes. Until you are able to see that Jesus is God with the assumed nature of man, you will never be able to understand His mediatorial High Priestly prayer in John 17.

To the Father Jesus said, "That they might know thee the only true God, and Jesus Christ, whom thou hast sent" (John 17:3).

If the Father is "the only true God," then all others would be false. In God's fatherhood He is separate and unmixed with alien or foreign substance, so that in His position as Father He is pure God. However, when God fused Himself with flesh and took the form of a servant and was called Jesus Christ, the admixture forbad the designation of Jesus Christ as being entirely God, free from extraneous ingredients. Hence, Jesus Christ, taken as a whole, is not purely or truly God since He is God-Man or God and Man in fusion, not confusion.

"And this is eternal life; to know you, the only true and real God, and to know Him, Jesus Christ, the Anointed One, the Messiah, Whom you have sent" (John 17:3 Amplified New Testament).

1 John 5:20 shows that Jesus is strictly God if you will view His divine nature as God.

Is this why the Son of God is also called the true God?

The Father is the only true God (John 17:3). The verse implied by the question is 1 John 5:20: "And we know that the Son of God is come, and hath given us an understanding, that we may know him that is true, and we are in him that is true, even in his Son Jesus Christ. This is the true God and eternal life."

Jesus Himself said that "life eternal" was to "know the only true God." These words were addressed to the Father, but Jesus continued by saying that they were to know "Jesus Christ, Whom Thou hast sent."

John said that the Son of God had come and had given an understanding to "us" that we may know Him (the Father) that is true." Now, He Who came and brought this understanding was the Son of God, and the Son must be true for us to believe He told the truth about God. He is called "the faithful and true witness" (Revelation 3:14). Of Himself He said, "I am the way, the truth, and the life; no man cometh unto the Father, but by me" (John 14:6).

Hence, we are in Him Who is True, yea, the truth concerning God, even in His Son (God's Son), Jesus Christ. This one we know is the true God and this Jesus Christ, as Son of God, is "eternal life" to know.

In 1 John 5:20 the writer is saying that the Son of God came to bear witness of the truth, and must Himself be the truth about the true God if He is to be believed. Hence, to be in Jesus Christ is to be in Him Who is true; but it is the only true God, called the Father, that is intended in this verse. To know the only true God, or God pure of any extraneous substance (such as flesh, blood, temptations, etc.) was the mission of Jesus, the Son; and we are in Him Who made us to know the only true God, even in His (the true God's) Son, Jesus Christ. The Deity in the Son is one undivided substance with the Father.

Jesus is God when His divinity is carefully considered apart from His humanity, but when He is thus contemplated, He is identical with and to the Father—one Substance, Divine.

God and Jesus are like an Idea and a Word. The idea is conveyed in the word. God is conveyed to man in the Word made flesh (Jesus Christ).

GOD AND JESUS CHRIST THE SAME

WHAT IN SUMMARY REVEALS THAT JESUS CHRIST, THE SON OF GOD, IS THE ONE GOD OF THE OLD TESTAMENT, MANIFESTED, REVEALED, AND EMBODIED IN THE FLESH?

"Therefore the Lord himself shall give you a sign;

Behold a virgin shall conceive, and bear a son, and shall call his name Immanuel'' (Isaiah 7:14). When Jesus was born, Matthew said that His birth fulfilled this prophecy; and that Immanuel (spelled Emmanuel Matthew 1:23) ''being interpreted is God with us.''

and

''For unto us a child is born, unto us a son is given: and the government shall be upon his shoulder: and His name shall be called Wonderful, Counsellor, The mighty God, The everlasting Father, The Prince of Peace'' (Isaiah 9:6). When this child was born, and this son was given, His name was called Jesus. The name Jesus is the same as JEHOVAH. Therefore, that Name included all these other terms that identify and describe God. Hence, Jesus is God with us—JEHOVAH or LORD GOD WITH US.

and

''But thou, Bethlehem Ephratah, though thou be little among the thousands of Judah, yet out of thee shall he come forth unto me that is to be ruler in Israel; whose goings forth have been from of old, from everlasting'' (Micah 5:2). This is the very passage quoted by the chief priests and scribes when Herod asked them where Christ (Messiah) should be born (Matthew 2). Messiah was to be that One Who was from Everlasting. Only God is from Everlasting.

and

''The Word was God. . .and the Word was made flesh and dwelt among us'' (John 1:1, 14).

and

''God was manifest in the flesh'' (1 Timothy 3:16).

and

''But unto the Son he saith, Thy throne O God, is for ever and ever'' (Hebrews 1:8).

and

"For in him [Jesus] dwelleth all the fulness of the Godhead bodily" (Colossians 2:9).

and

"I am Alpha and Omega, the beginning and the ending, saith the Lord, which is, and which was and which is to come, the Almighty" (Revelation 1:8).

with

Revelation 4:8, 9 where the One on the throne is described: "Holy, holy, holy, Lord God Almighty, which was, and is, and is to come. And when those beasts give glory and honour and thanks to him that sat on the throne, who liveth for ever and ever."

with

"And he that sat upon the throne said, Behold, I make all things new. And he said unto me, Write: for these words are true and faithful. And he said unto me, It is done. I am Alpha and Omega, the beginning and the end. I will give unto him that is athirst of the fountain of the water of life freely. He that overcometh shall inherit all things; and I will be his God, and he shall be my son" (Revelation 21:5-7).

Alpha and Omega is Jesus Christ (Revelation 1:9-18). He is the Almighty and is on this One Throne in heaven.

Until you will recognize God as an Omnipresent Spirit in His basic essence, and that His Impressed or Expressed Character is embodied in the flesh (the God-Man); and that Jesus Christ, the Son of God, is that One Omnipresent Invisible God made present in that particular body; and that the Holy Ghost is that measure of God that overshadowed Mary to impregnate her with LIFE (God's LIFE) and also fills believing human beings, you will for the rest of your life be fumbling with the arithmetical formula worked out by an Apostate Church during the centuries after the first one hundred years of the Church.

There remains no reason for any further blundering along that superstitious path cut out by men long departed from the doctrine, and practices of the Apostles and early Church.

"There is one God, and one mediator between God and men, the man Christ Jesus" (1 Timothy 2:5).

"A mediator is not a mediator of one, but God is one" (Galatians 3:20).

GOD, LORD and Lord

FROM WHAT WORD DO WE GET THE NAMES GOD, LORD AND Lord?

Elohim is the word from whence comes the English form "God." It is a uni-plural noun meaning strength and faithfulness. Nothing in the name expresses or implies a plurality of persons in any place in the Old Testament. It is a word used for a false god as well as the true God. It is used about two thousand five hundred times in the Old Testament.

WHAT IS THE MEANING OF THE NAME LORD IN THE OLD TESTAMENT?

LORD and JEHOVAH are synonyms. Jehovah is the Hebrew and is from Yahweh. It means the Self-existent One

Who continues to reveal Himself. The name God simply refers to the Strong and Faithful One. When LORD (Yahweh or Jehovah) is added and the term "LORD GOD" is used, then the Self Existent One, not Self Existent Three, reveals Himself.

It was the LORD GOD Who made heaven and earth (Genesis 2:4). It was the LORD GOD Who formed man of the dust of the ground and breathed into his nostrils the breath of life; and man became a living soul (Genesis 2:7).

LORD is the name of God. It is also His redemptive name (Genesis 8:9-13, 21, etc.); also His Covenant name.

In creation it was He, not Them, that made male and female in the beginning. Jesus said, "Have ye not read, that he which made them at the beginning made them male and female" (Matthew 19:4).

God is called He and male and female are called them. And "they twain shall be one flesh" (Matthew 19:5).

God's Oneness is not like the oneness of male and female, for the man and woman are called them and they, while God is called He.

The name LORD (Jehovah) is compounded with other names to show various relationships to man:

Jehovah-Jereh	—The LORD will provide (Genesis 22:13, 14)
Jehovah-rapha	—The LORD that healeth (Exodus 15:26)
Jehovah-nissi	—The LORD our banner (Exodus 17:8-15)
Jehovah-Shalom	—The LORD our peace (Judges 6:24)
Jehovah-ra-ah	—The LORD my shepherd (Psalms 23)

Jehovah-tsidkenu	—The LORD our righteousness (Jeremiah 23:6)
Jehovah-shammah	—The LORD is present (Ezekiel 48:35)

WHAT IS THE MEANING OF THE NAME Lord?

The spelling is with small letters and is from the Hebrew "Adonai" which means master and husband. It is a name for men as well as God. It is unto the Adonai that Jehovah said, "Sit thou at my right hand" (Psalm 110:1). This is not God speaking to God, but God is speaking of Jesus in His mediatorial capacity. "There is one God (Jehovah) and one Mediator between God and men, the man Christ Jesus" (1 Timothy 2:5).

It may be well to note here, however, that the Greek name "Jesus" is equivalent to the Hebrew name "Jehovah" (Yahweh). Thus, Jesus is not only man—He is Jehovah. Right hand is a figurative term and not a literal fact.

Did Jehovah or LORD say, "I am the Almighty God?" What is its significance?

Almighty God is what Jehovah claimed in identifying Himself and describing His omnipotence to Abram. Almighty God is from the Hebrew "El Shaddai". It is particularly interesting to note that Jesus Christ claimed to be "the Almighty" (Revelation 1:8).

If Jehovah and Jesus are the same, and there is One Jehovah, how can this be reconciled with the Trinitarian concept that each person in the Godhead is Jehovah?

Actually, there is no way to reconcile this pluralistic concept. "Hear, O Israel: The LORD (JEHOVAH) our

GOD (ELOHIM) is ONE LORD (JEHOVAH)."

In His Deity Jesus is the one Jehovah of the Old Testament. But in His humanity He is the Adonai of Psalms 110:1.

Do not think that Adonai necessarily is confined to a human ruler, for the term may also be connected with God. However, there exists a distinction in the terms.

WHAT IS IN A NAME?

There is a great deal of meaning in the name "Jesus." As heretofore stated, the name Jesus is the same as Jehovah except Jesus is Greek and Jehovah is Hebrew. God said that Jehovah was His name (Exodus 6:3).

If Jehovah is God's Old Testament name and Jesus means the same in Greek, it follows that God's name is Jesus. The name Jesus is, by inheritance, a more excellent name than any name borne by the angels (Hebrews 1:3, 4).

Jesus, in His humanity, was crucified; but in His resurrection was made both Lord and Christ.

The Hebrew words Adonai and Jehovah are spelled alike in the Greek language. Therefore, Lord could mean that Jesus is made Master or Husband over all by His resurrection; and as Christ, He is anointed above His fellows.

In summary, Lord could possibly refer to the Adonai of Psalm 110:1 and not to the Jehovah of Psalms 110:1. Christ or Messiah is anointed above all other of his fellows (Moses, Aaron, David, etc.).

Hence, Lord Jesus Christ, in all likelihood, is Adonai Jehovah Messiah (or Lord LORD MESSIAH). Thus, embracing the Old Testament names in Himself as a compound name.

THE NAME

IS THERE ANY SCRIPTURE OR SCRIPTURES THAT WILL SHOW THAT THERE IS A NAME COMMON TO THE TOTAL DEITY, WHETHER IN THE UNIVERSE, IN CHRIST, OR IN THE CHURCH?

Certainly.

"For unto us a child is born, unto us a son is given: and the government shall be upon his shoulder; and his name shall be called Wonderful, Counsellor, The mighty God, The everlasting Father, The Prince of Peace" (Isaiah 9:6).

This verse does not say His names shall be Wonderful, Counsellor, The Mighty God, The Everlasting Father or The Prince of Peace.

It does say, however, His NAME (whatsoever that name may be) will describe or will be called Wonderful, Counsellor, The Mighty God, The Everlasting Father, The Prince of Peace.

What was the Name of this child and son which means the various things in Isaiah 9:6? Jesus! (Matthew 1:21). The name Jesus means Wonderful, Counsellor, The Mighty God, The Everlasting Father, The Prince of Peace.

Words are names that identify and/or describe. Isaiah 9:6 reveals that the Name of this child will be a symbol that identifies as well as describes the Lord Jesus Christ as to Who and What He is.

You will recall that the Son, by inheritance, obtained a more excellent name than the angels. His name, Jesus, is the Greek synonym for the Hebrew Jehovah. When He said, "I am come in my Father's name" (John 5:43), He meant in the actual name, not merely by the authority only. He further said, "and ye received me not; if another shall come in his own name, him ye will receive" (John 5:43).

It is tremendously important that the name of Jesus should be stressed and not watered down by rationalizing. John said, "But these are written that ye might believe that Jesus is the Christ, the Son of God; and that believing ye might have life through his name" (John 20:31).

"And whatsoever ye shall ask in my name, that will I do, that the *Father* may be glorified in the son. If ye ask any thing in my name, I will do it" (John 14:13, 14).

"But the Comforter, which is the Holy Ghost, whom the Father will send in my name" (John 14:26 and also John 16:23, 24).

The Common Name Bond is JESUS.

JESUS CHRIST DESCRIBED

WHAT ARE SOME OF THE IDENTIFYING AND DESCRIPTIVE TERMS RELATED TO JESUS CHRIST?

His name is Jesus (Matthew 1:21). Jesus is the Greek synonym for Jehovah.

His name is Emmanuel (Matthew 1:23). Emmanuel means God With Us.

He is called King of the Jews (Matthew 27:37).

He is called The Lion of the Tribe of Judah (Revelation 5:5).

He is called The Lamb of God (John 1:29).

He is called High Priest after the order of Melchizidek. Melchizidek was a King-Priest (Hebrews 7).

He is called God (Hebrews 1:8).

He is called Son of God (1 John 4:15).

He is called Son of Man (John 3:13).

He is called The only begotten of the Father (John 1:14).

He is called God's beloved Son (Matthew 3:17).

He is called "Temple" (John 2:19).

He is called "Tent" or Tabernacle (John 1:14).

He is called Shepherd (John 10).

He is called The Door (John 10).

He is called The Way (John 14:6).

He is called The Truth (John 14:6).

He is called The Life (John 14:6).

He is called Christ (John 4:25).

He is called Savior (Luke 2:11).

He is called Lord (Philippians 2:11).

He is called the Bread of Life (John 6).

He is called The Light of the World (John 8:12).

He is called The Word (John 1:1; Revelation 19:13).

He is called The Image of God (Colossians 1:15).

He is called Advocate (1 John 2:1).

He is called King of Kings (Revelation 17:14).

He is called Lord of Lords (Revelation 17:14).

He is called Lord of All (Acts 10:36).

He is called God over all (Romans 9:5).

He is called That Blessed Hope (Titus 2:13).

He is called The Great God (Titus 2:13).

He is called Alpha and Omega (Revelation 1:8).

He is called The Almighty (Revelation 1:8).

He is called Mediator (1 Timothy 2:5).

He said, "I and My Father are One" (John 10:30).

He is called Creator (Hebrews 1:10).

He is called The Firstborn (Colossians 1:15).

He is called Son of David (Matthew 1:1).

He is called Son of Abraham (Matthew 1:1).

He is identified as "God manifest in the flesh (1 Timothy 3:16).

He is called a Prophet (Acts 7:37).

He is called This Rock (Matthew 16:18).

He is called The Chief Cornerstone (Acts 4:11).

He is The Head of the Church (Ephesians 1:20-22).

He is Before All things (Colossians 1:15-17).

By Him all Things Consist (Colossians 1:15-17).

He is The Impressed Character of God's Substance (Hebrews 1:3).

He is the form of God (Philippians 2:6).

He was made in the likeness of men (Philippians 2:6-8).

Is God on the One Throne in Heaven (Revelation 21:5-7).

Is called The LORD (JEHOVAH our Righteousness Jeremiah 23:6).

ONE NAME

ISN'T LORD JESUS CHRIST MORE THAN ONE NAME JUST AS FATHER, SON, AND HOLY GHOST ARE MORE THAN ONE NAME?

The difference lies in the object or objects being identified. In the last commission, Jesus commissioned His disciples to "Go ye therefore, and teach all nations, baptizing them in the name of the Father, and of the Son, and of the Holy Ghost" (Matthew 28:19).

If one views this verse as an identification of three separate and distinct objects of thought, it is clearly three names. However, Jesus said to baptize in the *Name of, not names of.*

The compound name is Lord Jesus Christ.

In short, a person may have the name of John Paul Jones. When the person is spoken to, or of, by his full name or any combination of John, John Jones, Paul, Paul Jones or John Paul Jones, it is merely a variation of the name.

If we say, Baptize in the name of the Father, and of the Husband, and of the Cousin, the emphasis is on the name of whoever this father, husband and cousin is. If John Paul Jones fits the description, then the name to baptize in is the name of John Paul Jones.

From the way the disciples baptized the early Christians, it is crystal clear that they always commanded and/or baptized into the name of the Lord Jesus Christ or variations of that compound name (Acts 2:38, 8:16, 10:48, 19:5, Romans 6:3, 4).

You see, even though God quantitatively transcends the body of Jesus Christ, yet the Father was in the Son (John 17:21), the Holy Ghost was in Jesus (Luke 4:1), and He, of course, was the Son. The three manifestations, descriptions, or even identifications headed up in Jesus Christ regardless of the extension of the Deity in Omnipresence. When we are buried with Him by baptism, we are baptized in to Jesus Christ with all that implies.

Many pluralists fail to see that all that God is, qualitatively, whether Father (source), the Son (means) or Holy Ghost (impartation) is seen in the Lord Jesus Christ. There is an interpenetration of the Godhead. Even though God quantitatively is also exterior to the body of Jesus Christ, this in no way means to omit or ignore any of the Deity. The Father, Son and Holy Ghost are one in Jesus Christ. The name of the total Godhead is Lord Jesus Christ—the name "Jesus," in particular, is God's name!

GOD ALL AND IN ALL

WILL THE SON DELIVER UP THE KINGDOM TO THE FATHER?

Of course. The Father is God in every sphere and dimension. The Son is the product of a fusion of God with man. The Father is God in His Omnipresence, and is the source from whence the Divine Life was united with human life in the virgin womb.

God could, in a sense, die in the mask or person of this

assumed human nature.

Because of man came death—because of man came also the resurrection of the dead. For as in Adam all die, even so in Christ shall all be made alive (1 Corinthians 15:21, 22).

This particular projection of God in a Son was to destroy all enemies—the last enemy being death. God in particular is in Christ manifest in order to gather all things in one so that God in His entirety may be all in all (1 Corinthians 15:24-28).

Hence, in the ultimate end, God in His unlimited quantity and absolute infinity will be Sovereign. The purpose of the Sonship will have been served, and the total rule of God in His Omnipresence will take the place of the rule of God in a Son—His Particular Presence. The Sonship will not cease, but the particularity will flow over into God's Eternality and Generality. Then God in all His Power, Honor, Glory and Kingdom will be all and in all (1 Corinthians 15:28).

There will be no veil of time and space or sin and death. God in His Wholeness and Entirety will prevail in a limitless eternity after the end of time. All limits as are now known will be off. We will not only know God in Christ, but God exterior to Christ. God interior or exterior to Christ is the same, but the heighth, depth, length and width of Deity will be in Absolute charge in complete and uninhibited freedom and righteousness.

There will be no devil, no sin, no death and no conflict. God will be all in all.

Yes, "When all things shall be subdued unto him, then shall the Son [on His human side will] also himself be subject unto him that put all things under him, that God may be all in all" (1 Corinthians 15:28).

CONCLUSION

WHAT CAN WE SAY ABOUT JESUS CHRIST?

He is God and man united. As man Jesus possessed body (Hebrews 10:5), soul (Isaiah 53:10-12; Matthew 26:38; Acts 2:27, 31), and spirit or ghost (Luke 23:46).

As God Jesus is the quintessence of God. He is God's FORM and essence extracted or drawn from the Divine Substance. He is God highly concentrated in a body. He is God's essential FORM properties, or essence or nature embodied.

He is God and Man in unity. This was done through the miracle of the virgin birth. This is how God and Man interpenetrated. This is why Jesus is often times called the God-Man.

As God on earth Jesus is God delimited from His former glory. He is God's Word-Image confined within a body. He is God living within the scope of human life and many other limits that are seen in the life, trials, and death of Jesus Christ.

At the same time Jesus as man was freed from many of the limits of man, i.e. He was tempted, but did not sin; He defeated the devil at every turn; by faith He conquered the world. Though Jesus was tempted, it was not due to inward lust and pride. And He thus brought hope to all men every where. If you want to reach the Father, take another look at Jesus Christ (John 14:6-11).

Under the chapter entitled Father and Lord, God the Father and the Lord Jesus Christ are set side by side language wise. Only the Father is called God. Why? Because the Deity of Jesus Christ is God; or God extended into human life through the Virgin birth. But since this which is born is the product of a union of two natures not heretofore known in that relation, the Son has therefore a Deity side.

Sonship is therefore a term used to identify a result of two natures fused through the Virgin birth. There is One God The Father, thus the Divine Nature in Jesus Christ is God extended into this world by means of the Virgin birth. This accounts for the Son being called God as the mind is directed back to God in contradistinction to His fusion with human nature.

Of course this God in Christ extends back into the Omnipresence as the heart reaches for the Father in Christ.

The Holy Ghost is the Father extended to the bodies and souls of human kind. So that God in Christ or in the church is the Father extended to other spheres other than space, time, and eternity.

Jesus Christ is God's Word-Image, Shape, or Form (John 20:28), inside human form.

The term God-Man as applied in this book, does not mean to this author, a confusion of the two natures (Divine and Human) in Jesus Christ. But the union of the two natures is more and different than two persons holding hands in one body. The distinction is: Jesus Christ was born with four elements instead of three—He had body, soul, and spirit (as have we) plus the Word. And just as the soul and human spirit in man are in connection, yet can be distinguished (Hebrews 4:12; 1 Thessalonians 5:23), so the Word incarnate is not absorbed and lost in Jesus Christ. But rather He possessed two natures alloyed together by means of the Virgin Birth.

The End